SpringerBriefs in Business

SpringerBriefs present concise summaries of cutting-edge research and practical applications across a wide spectrum of fields. Featuring compact volumes of 50 to 125 pages, the series covers a range of content from professional to academic. Typical topics might include:

- A timely report of state-of-the art analytical techniques
- A bridge between new research results, as published in journal articles, and a contextual literature review
- A snapshot of a hot or emerging topic
- An in-depth case study or clinical example
- A presentation of core concepts that students must understand in order to make independent contributions

SpringerBriefs in Business showcase emerging theory, empirical research, and practical application in management, finance, entrepreneurship, marketing, operations research, and related fields, from a global author community.

Briefs are characterized by fast, global electronic dissemination, standard publishing contracts, standardized manuscript preparation and formatting guidelines, and expedited production schedules.

Wim Vandekerckhove

Whistleblowing Management Systems and Speak-Up Cultures

Alignment with International Standards and Requirements

Springer

Wim Vandekerckhove
EDHEC Business School
Lille, France

ISSN 2191-5482 ISSN 2191-5490 (electronic)
SpringerBriefs in Business
ISBN 978-3-032-14203-0 ISBN 978-3-032-14204-7 (eBook)
https://doi.org/10.1007/978-3-032-14204-7

This work was supported by European Commission.

This Springer imprint is published by the registered company Springer Nature Switzerland AG
The registered company address is: Gewerbestrasse 11, 6330 Cham, Switzerland

For Quinten, Laurens, and Francine.

Contents

About the Author

Wim Vandekerckhove is (Full) Professor of Business Ethics at EDHEC Business School in France. He holds a Ph.D. from Ghent University. Before joining EDHEC, he has held academic affiliations to Ghent University (Belgium), the University of Oslo (Norway), Griffith University (Australia), the International Anti-Corruption Academy (Austria), and the University of Greenwich (UK). Wim has been Editor-in-Chief for *Philosophy of Management*, and is currently Consulting Editor for the *Journal of Business Ethics*.

Wim has provided expertise to various organizations, including Council of Europe, United Nations Office on Drugs and Crime (UNODC), the International Olympic Committee (IOC), Transparency International, the UK Department of Health, the UK Financial Conduct Authority. He is a committee member of the British Standards Institute (BSI) on governance. He led the development of ISO37002:2021, the international standard for Whistleblowing Management Systems, and participated in developing BS25700 Organizational Responses to Modern Slavery.

Chapter 1
Introduction

Abstract This chapter states the aim of the book, namely to help integrity professionals improve current practices in handling whistleblowing reports and build speak-up cultures in organizations. It explains that the book cannot convince people to want to manage whistleblowing channels in support of speak-up cultures, but that good will alone is no guarantee for good outcomes. This book draws on research to points at some pitfalls to avoid as well as some ways to make change happen. The chapter also sketches the structure of the book and mentions the EU-funded project that this book is part of BRIGHT (EACEA101143423).

This book is about organizational whistleblowing systems and speak-up cultures. It aims to help improve current practice in handling whistleblowing reports. Organizational whistleblowing systems involve internal channels for members and stakeholders of an organization to report a concern about wrongdoing. What makes a channel internal is not where the report starts or runs through, but where it ends. Some parts of an internal whistleblowing channel may be outsourced, for example to a service company that provides the web or mobile interface or who does initial triage of the reports. At some point however, reports will go back inside the organization, where someone is mandated to make further follow-up decisions. Thus, although technically the whistleblowing channel has external features, legally and de facto, it is an internal channel.

The pivoting movement in this book is that a well-managed whistleblowing system can help build speak-up cultures. Yet this book is not a good news show. The data this book draws on suggests that in general, organizations are not good in managing their internal channels as a whistleblowing system. They leave many opportunities to build culture unused, or remain blind to the confusing signals they send about their whistleblowing channels. This book aims to help integrity professionals and scholars see these untapped opportunities and mistakes.

Of course, in some organizations the climate is to 'put up and shut up', without any intention to listen to whistleblowers. Indeed, some companies are run by crooks, and internal whistleblowing will never work out well in there. But that is a tiny minority of organizations. In any case, this book is not for them. At the other end of

W. Vandekerckhove, *Whistleblowing Management Systems and Speak-Up Cultures*, SpringerBriefs in Business, https://doi.org/10.1007/978-3-032-14204-7_1

the spectrum, there are organizations that have nurtured excellent speak-up cultures and their integrity professionals have vast experience in running internal channels in support of their speak-up cultures. I hope these integrity professionals can agree with the analysis and guidance I present here, but I don't think they will find anything they do not know yet in this book. But that is also a tiny minority.

For the vast majority of organizations however, this book can be useful. Over the past years I have encountered many integrity professionals and managers who seemed to want to do a better job at handling whistleblowing reports and who acknowledged their organization's cultures needed higher levels of trust, but simply had no clue as to how they could go about making the change happen. This book is for them. You have to want to do the right thing, but good will alone is no guarantee for a good outcome. This book points at some pitfalls to avoid as well as some ways to make change happen.

This book is part of a project funded by the European Union, in promoting the EU Whistleblowing Directive (2019/1937) and to facilitate an improved environment for successful whistleblowing. The project is called BRIGHT (EACEA101143234) and spans March 2024 to February 2026. Project partners are EDHEC Business School, the European Whistleblowing Institute, and the University of Galway. I am grateful to Kate Kenny, Taymi Milan, Vigjilenca Abazi, Bruno Galizzi, Lauren Kierans, Dimitrios Kafteranis, and Caterina Vila Nova for the collaboration on the project. At EDHEC, I coordinated the project. My own work package in the project consisted of developing SUSA, a free online and anonymous tool that allows integrity professional to self-assess how well their internal whistleblowing systems align with the EU requirements, ISO37002:2021, and the 2022 ICC Guidelines. For SUSA, I was fortunate to be able to work with Sonny Luypaert, Koen Albers, Beata Baran, Valvanera Campos, Hugh Penri-Williams, Evi Dimitroulia, Douglas Linares Flinto, and Andrew Samuels.

This book draws on my research into whistleblowing processes. It draws on data from SUSA and also other research projects. More precisely, work on signaling trustworthiness I did with Kate Kenny, Mariana Fotaki, and Didem Derya Özdemir Kaya. I also present here a re-analysis of data I collected in a research project I did with Nataliya Rumyantseva. I learned a lot from collaborating with these scholars.

The book is structured as follows. The next chapter focuses on the quality of whistleblowing systems. It starts by drawing best practice guidance from three normative benchmarks: the 2022 ICC Guidelines on whistleblowing, the ISO37002:2021 standard, and the requirements for internal whistleblowing systems in the EU Whistleblowing Directive (2019/1937). The chapter also explains how to use the SUSA tool to self-assess how well an organization aligns with these benchmarks. Finally, the chapter presents some research based on the SUSA data around governance indicators of whistleblowing systems.

Chapter three makes the pivot from channels and handling processes to cultures of trust. It starts by using further SUSA data to show where organizations leave opportunities untapped to create more trustworthy whistleblowing systems and cultures of trust. The chapter then proceeds to analyze why integrity professionals tend to struggle making the organizational whistleblowing channels trustworthy.

In chapter four a deep dive is made into cognitive barriers for speak-up cultures. I analyze how integrity professionals make sense of the whistleblowing channels and of whistleblowers to identify two sets of epistemological and axiological assumptions, one of listeners and another set of those who disperse others' speak-up.

I conclude the book by summarizing the key points made throughout the chapters, pivoting from operating formal channels for people to speak up, to subconscious biases toward those who speak up. I am grateful to the many whistleblowers I was able to meet in my work on whistleblowing. Some of them have become friends. This book is not about the whistleblowers. Rather, the book is about our repeated failures to listen to them. It is written in the hope we might get better at listening.

Wim Vandekerckhove is (Full) Professor of Business Ethics at EDHEC Business School in France. He holds a PhD from Ghent University. Before joining EDHEC, he has held academic affiliations to Ghent University (Belgium), the University of Oslo (Norway), Griffith University (Australia), the International Anti-Corruption Academy (Austria), and the University of Greenwich (UK). Wim has been Editor-in-Chief for *Philosophy of Management*, and is currently Consulting Editor for the *Journal of Business Ethics*. Wim has provided expertise to various organizations, including Council of Europe, United Nations Office on Drugs and Crime (UNODC), the International Olympic Committee (IOC), Transparency International, the UK Department of Health, the UK Financial Conduct Authority. He is a committee member of the British Standards Institute (BSI) on governance. He led the development of ISO37002:2021, the international standard for Whistleblowing Management Systems, and participated in developing BS25700 Organizational Responses to Modern Slavery.

Chapter 2
Normative Benchmarks and Current SUSA Practice

Abstract This chapter focuses on the quality of whistleblowing systems. It starts by drawing best practice guidance from three normative benchmarks: the 2022 ICC Guidelines on whistleblowing, the ISO37002:2021 standard, and the requirements for internal whistleblowing systems in the EU Whistleblowing Directive (2019/1937). The chapter also explains how to use the SUSA tool to self-assess how well an organization aligns with these benchmarks. Finally, the chapter presents some research based on the SUSA data around governance indicators of whistleblowing systems.

2.1 Guidance from Normative Benchmarks

This section provides guidance for operating effective whistleblowing channels in organizations. It is written with a specific audience in mind, namely integrity professionals. This includes anyone who is tasked with designing, implementing, operating, or overseeing whistleblowing channels in organizations.

The guidance presented here can be used in conjunction with SUSA, the Speak-Up Self-Assessment tool described further in this chapter, which can be used to see how an organizational whistleblowing channel aligns with ISO37002:2021, the 2022 ICC Guidelines, and the requirements of the EU Directive (2019/1937). The guidance in this chapter also uses those benchmarks. The expertise used to build SUSA and write the guidance in this section was developed through working with whistleblowers, integrity professionals, civil society organizations, and policymakers.

In December 2019, the EU Whistleblowing Directive came into force after its publication in the Official Journal of the European Union. Its full title is 'Directive (EU) 2019/1937 of the European Parliament and of the Council of 23 October 2019 on the protection of persons who report breaches of Union law', but it is widely known as the *EU Whistleblowing Directive (2019/1937)*.[1] It had taken quite some debates and maneuvering to get it there (see my discussion in Vandekerckhove, 2022). However, in the EU a Directive needs to be transposed into the national legislation of the EU Member States, usually within two years. In this case, that

[1] See https://eur-lex.europa.eu/eli/dir/2019/1937/oj/eng.

W. Vandekerckhove, *Whistleblowing Management Systems and Speak-Up Cultures*, SpringerBriefs in Business, https://doi.org/10.1007/978-3-032-14204-7_2

took a bit longer but by September 2024 all Member States had adopted the required transposition law. Nevertheless, some areas of the transposition remained inadequate (Del Monte & Faucheux, 2024). While the EU Whistleblowing Directive requires Member States to mandate competent authorities to receive and handle reports from whistleblowers, it also requires organizations in both public and private sectors to have internal whistleblowing channels. It is these requirements that are used as a benchmark for the guidance in this chapter.

The International Chamber of Commerce (ICC) is one of the largest and most representative business organization in the world. It represents large and small businesses in more than 170 countries, spanning every industry in the private sector. In 2008, the ICC published its first set of guidelines for companies to establish and implement internal whistleblowing channels. Recently, these were updated and published as the *ICC 2022 Guidelines on Whistleblowing.*[2] These guidelines are explicitly linked to the *ICC Rules on Combating Corruption.* In the update, the ICC has aligned its definitions and guidance to that of the ISO37002:2021 standard on whistleblowing management systems.

The International Organization for Standardization (ISO) was founded in 1947 as an independent international body to facilitate global collaboration and trade by developing and publishing a wide range of standards. Today, it has 173 national standard bodies as members. National standard bodies can initiate a proposal within ISO for the development of a particular standard. If approved by other national standard bodies, the ISO brings experts from different countries and different stakeholder categories together to develop consensus around a product or process. That becomes an ISO standard. The *ISO37002:2021 Whistleblowing Management Systems—Guidelines* is the international standard for internal whistleblowing systems. It provides guidelines for establishing, implementing, and maintaining whistleblowing channels and handling processes. The standard is intended to be applicable to organizations of all sizes and types, in all sectors and across activities. The standard was published in 2021.[3] I led the ISO working group that developed the standard, which took three years. In all, more than 160 experts from 35 countries across all continents and 7 liaison bodies participated in the development of this standard. We had many people from the compliance profession that participated, and also from government regulators, labor unions, civil society, as well as whistleblowers. I am proud of the result. The best way to describe ISO37002:2021 is, I believe, as an international multi-stakeholder consensus of what best practice in handling whistleblowing reports looks like.

I have used ISO37002:2021 as a framework in my research, in developing SUSA, and also a couple of times in some consultancy work. It is a very useful framework to identify what is already happening, what needs improvement, and what concrete things can be done to improve. That has been my inspiration to write the guidance in this chapter. Each section covers specific aspects of a whistleblowing management

---

[2] See https://iccwbo.org/news-publications/policies-reports/icc-2022-guidelines-on-whistleblowing/.

[3] See https://www.iso.org/standard/65035.html#lifecycle.

system. In writing it, I am deliberately avoiding the technical or legal tone that you will find in the ISO37002:2021 or the EU Whistleblowing Directive. The ICC Guidelines are an easy entry for anyone, but sometimes lack a bit of detail. I have tried to distil the gist of each of the three benchmarks into the next couple of sub-sections. For each, I indicate where in the ICC Guidelines sections, the ISO37002:2021 sections, and the Articles of the EU Whistleblowing Directive you can find further detail.

2.1.1 Whistleblowing Channels and Feedback

Normative references include

- ISO37002:2021 sections 4.3, 8.1, 8.2, 8.3.1
- EU Directive 2019/1937 Art. 2, 6.2, 8.2, 9.1, 9.2, 18.2, 18.3, 18.4
- ICC sections ‘Whistleblowing Management System’, ‘Scope’

Which channels are good?

The EU requires every legal entity that has 50 or more workers to operate a whistleblowing channel. It is hard to say what channels will work best in your organization. But regardless of size, structure, sector, and culture, the following principles apply.

Have more than one channel. Consider channels with different technological interfaces (face-to-face, email, phone, app, online) to accommodate personal preferences. Also consider having people on the other end that potential whistleblowers could feel comfortable with for reporting wrongdoing. If you do not have a default face-to-face channel, the EU requires that whistleblowers can ask for a physical meeting to make their report.

Avoid having too many channels because that might get confusing. Take care not to slice up your channels for specific types of wrongdoing. Whistleblowers are not supposed to do the work in deciding how their report needs to be followed-up on. Do not expect whistleblowing reports to come clean and neatly identifying one specific type of wrongdoing. And don’t throw away a report because it was not made through the proper channel.

Whatever whistleblowing channels you operate, you must be able to register every report made, document decisions made in following-up these reports, and ensure the confidentiality throughout the process. If you make an audio-recording of a report, you must keep the recording or transcribe it. If you make a transcript, you must give the whistleblower the opportunity to check, rectify, and confirm this transcript. If you do not audio-record a report, you must keep minutes of the report, and give the whistleblower the opportunity to check, rectify, and agree with these minutes. A face-to-face (or physical) meeting can be audio-recorded or minutes can be taken.

Make the most of the technological possibilities of your channels to increase the ease-of-access for your potential whistleblowers. Different interfaces have various advantages, for example: availability for multiple languages, 24/7 availability, two-way anonymous interaction, uploading attachments, accompanied reporting, and reporting as part of a broader conversation.

For each channel, seek ways to inform the whistleblower about what they can expect and what they can do once they have reported the wrongdoing. The EU obliges Member States to make information available about advice and assistance for whistleblowers. You can at least point them toward that information, as well as reference the relevant whistleblowing legislation (national and EU). You can also inform them about when they can expect a response from you, and what the operational provisions and limitations are on confidentiality and protection.

No EU Member State currently forbids entities to operate channels that make anonymous reports possible. In any case, you will receive anonymous reports of wrongdoing. The EU has left it to Member States whether entities are obliged to follow-up on anonymous reports. But why would you not do so? If you believe that anonymous reports are less credible, then remember that a report itself is never evidence, but any report can lead you to find evidence of wrongdoing.

Who can use the whistleblowing channels?

It is best to think very broadly on this question and consider everyone who interacts with your organization. The EU requires that, at a minimum, anyone who performs work for your organization under any kind of contract can use your whistleblowing channels to report wrongdoing. This includes:

- Full-time, part-time, and temporary employees, self-employed and agency workers
- Interns and trainees, paid or unpaid
- Managers and directors, including non-executive directors
- Volunteers
- Shareholders
- Anyone working for a contractor, subcontractor, or supplier.

What can people use the whistleblowing channels for?

The EU has sought to legislate for whistleblowing on breaches of EU law, which relates to public procurement, financial services, product safety, transport safety, environment, nuclear safety, food safety, animal health, public health, consumer protection, privacy and personal data. National laws can make this even broader.

The best advice for organizations is not to be too worried about the scope of the whistleblowing legislation. Rather, a whistleblowing channel can help an organization find any kind of wrongdoing it risks happening under its responsibility, and therefore any kind of wrongdoing it might be complicit to. For an organization, the best scope for its whistleblowing channel is at least as wide as any breach of organizational policy or code of conduct.

What is good feedback?

When a whistleblower uses your whistleblowing channel to report wrongdoing, they expect you to look into the issue and take action to stop the wrongdoing. You might be doing all that, but if you do not give any feedback the whistleblower might believe you are doing nothing, and lose trust in you.

Feedback is a broad concept. It includes any indication that the whistleblowing report is being handled and taken seriously. The EU requires you to acknowledge receiving the whistleblowing report within seven days and give some information on how the report was handled within three months. But that might be too little too late.

The ISO 37002:2021 standard sees giving feedback as a way to maintain trust throughout the handling process. A channel can be set up to immediately give an automated acknowledgement of receipt, and this can be followed up with a personalized message a couple of days later. At each step of the handling process, feedback messages can include: what the next steps are, what possible outcomes are, timeframe for next steps, reasons for limited detail of feedback, information about available support and protection measures.

If you can, a follow-up with 'how are you now?' can be an important message for someone who is anxious about whistleblowing and possible reactions.

2.1.2 Follow-Up and Handling Process

Normative references include:

- ISO 37002:2021 sections 4.3, 7.5, 7.5.3, 7.5.5, 8.3.1, 8.3.2, 8.4.1, 8.5
- EU Directive 2019/1937 Art 16.1
- ICC section 'Roles and responsibilities', 'Management of the report'

Every whistleblowing report must be followed-up on, i.e., you need to do something with it according to a documented process. This is done through the handling process, which consists of: receiving a report, triage, and further actions. The triage is where you determine how a whistleblowing report will be handled, and further actions can include: asking more information, investigating, initiating protection, or referring to another procedure.

What defines good triage?

The aim of triage, or a first assessment of a report, is not to decide whether or not to investigate. Rather, the aim of triage is to find out how to best follow-up a whistleblowing report. Useful aspects to consider include:

- What is the nature of the reported wrongdoing? (type, frequency, has it happened or will it happen, role and seniority of alleged wrongdoer)
- Was there an earlier report of the same or similar wrongdoing?
- Are there immediate risks to human rights, safety, the environment?
- Is there an immediate need to protect evidence?

- Is it a criminal offence or something else that implies a duty to inform the authorities?
- Are there risks to organizational functions or reputation?
- What is the risk to the whistleblower?

The outcome of triage can be to ask the whistleblower for more information, to start an investigation into the alleged wrongdoing, to initiate protection measures in communication with the whistleblower, to inform the authorities, etc.

What is important when investigating?

Conducting a proper investigation is not that simple and easy. In many countries you need appropriately qualified individuals to convey legitimacy to an investigation.

In any case, the investigation needs to be trustworthy for all parties involved, so you must avoid any actual or perceived bias. It is therefore useful to consider engaging external investigators.

Credible investigations have a well-defined scope and terms-of-reference—what, who, when, how, why—and should be adequately resourced.

And of course, the investigation is carried out so that it protects evidence and protects the confidentiality of whistleblower and alleged wrongdoer.

How can a case be closed?

Closing the handling of a whistleblowing report means you have reached a finding about the whistleblowing report. If there was not enough information and the whistle-blower could not be reached then this can be noted in the records. If it was referred to another procedure this too can be documented.

If there has been an investigation, findings are reached and documented. This will need to go to others in the organization to decide on further actions. Leadership commitment to follow-up on the findings of an investigation is key to effective internal whistleblowing channels.

Closing the handling process involves making recommendations to leaders for further action on: disciplinary actions, continuing protection measures, lessons learned, and the need for policy review.

At closing stage, decisions will need to be made on data retention and whether this case can be used for organizational learning.

If wrongdoing was found, leaders will need to decide on measures to correct the wrongdoing as well as how to monitor the effectiveness of these measures. There might also be a legal duty to inform authorities.

You will also give feedback to the whistleblower at this stage. If wrongdoing was found, there might be legal restrictions on how much detail you can provide about evidence and sanctions. That is why you need to inform the whistleblower at an earlier stage about these restrictions. If wrongdoing was not substantiated, it is just as important to provide feedback, explaining the lack of evidence or why the whistleblower's perception of wrongdoing might have been mistaken.

2.1.3 Protection and Remedy

Normative references include:

- ISO 37002:2021 sections 8.4.2, 8.4.3
- EU Directive 2019/1937 Art. 19, 21, 22
- ICC section 'Non-retaliation'

Protection against what?

You have to protect a whistleblower against any act or omission prompted by the whistleblowing report, that leads to or could lead to harm to the whistleblower. It is best to understand this in a broad sense: the harm can be intentional or unintentional, the whistleblowing can be the main cause of the harm, one of the causes, or merely have contributed to the harm. Finally, the whistleblowing can be anticipated. For example, if someone said they will report the wrongdoing and are fired before they make the report.

It is also best to understand 'harm' in a broad sense: professional, financial, physical, and psychological.

What can be done as pro-active protection?

You will be better at protecting whistleblowers if you have a documented set of protection measures and action plans to activate these protection measures. Any measure will have limitations depending on what your organization looks like and what the working relationship is with the whistleblower (for example, your own employee or an agency worker). Developing a documented set of protection measures will help you become aware of these limitations.

Consider protection measures before harm occurs. At the triage stage you can assess the risk of retaliation:

- How difficult will it be to keep the whistleblower's identity confidential?
- Who else knows about the wrongdoing?
- Is the whistleblower involved in the wrongdoing or are they the target?
- Who would seek retaliation?
- Does the whistleblower expect retaliation? From whom?
- What is the relationship between whistleblower and alleged wrongdoer?
- Is the whistleblower in a vulnerable situation? (for example, are they a young person, migrant worker, have a disability, or other characteristic or administrative status)
- What can be done as pro-active and re-active protection?

When a whistleblower indicates they have suffered harm, presume that harm was in relation to their whistleblowing, unless there is convincing evidence that there are other reasons unrelated to their whistleblowing. Investigations into retaliation must be carried out by persons that have no conflict of interest.

If there is no convincing evidence that the harm was unrelated to the whistleblowing, this harm to the whistleblower must be remedied.

What does remedy involve?

The whistleblower must be financially compensated for damages they have suffered.

A written or public apology to the whistleblower by management can be very meaningful for a whistleblower.

You have to restore the whistleblower's situation to conditions had they not suffered harm. For example in terms of:

- Position in the organization, reputation, salary, responsibilities.
- Access to training, promotion, benefits, entitlements.
- Any litigation against the whistleblower must be withdrawn.

2.1.4 Data Management and Confidentiality

Normative references include:

- ISO 37002:2021 sections 7.5.3, 7.5.4, 7.5.5
- EU Directive 2019/1937 Art 9.1, 16.1, 17, 18.1
- EU Regulation 2016/679 Art. 9, 12, 13.1, 14.5, 15, 16, 17, 18, 19, 35
- ICC section 'Management of the report'

The organization needs to have a data management plan for its internal whistleblowing channel and handling process. The plan must allow the organization to control information so that it is adequately protected, and is available for use (for investigation, review, monitoring, accountability). It is best to develop this in line with a privacy impact assessment, to establish how the privacy risks associated with the handling process can be managed.

A data management plan needs to address: what data is stored, about who data is stored, how the data is stored, who has access and can use the data, control of changes, retention and disposition of data.

What records need to be kept?

You have to keep records of all whistleblowing reports, actions taken (triage, protection, sanctions, informing authorities), and outcomes of investigation.

You should not store these records longer than necessary, but that does not mean you can simply delete everything. Once the handling of a case is closed, you need to consider what is still necessary in light of continued protection measures, or pending judicial steps.

It is specifically personal data that needs to be taken care of. Personal data includes the identity of a person or data that, in combination, can identify a person.

Analyzing organizational trends and learning will not require personal data to be kept but makes categorization and some level of detail necessary, also drawing from the whistleblowing reports that did not entail enough information to warrant an investigation.

Avoid the collection of personal data that is obviously not relevant for handling a specific whistleblowing report. If such data is accidentally collected it must be deleted as soon as possible.

In case sensitive data is mentioned in a report specific processing conditions should be implemented. Examples of sensitive data include personal data revealing racial or ethnic origin, political opinions, religious or philosophical beliefs, trade-union membership, genetic data, biometric data processed solely to identify a human being, health-related data, data concerning a person's sex life or sexual orientation.

What do people need to know about how data is stored?

Information needs to be easily accessible in clear and plain language about:

- What personal data is stored, for how long, and for what purposes (period and criteria).
- How confidentiality is protected (and what the limitations are).
- Whether it is transferred to a non-EU country or international organization.
- Who the data controller (entity) and the data protection officer (contact) is.
- What their rights are (seeing, correcting, restricting, and deleting data).

2.1.5 What does the duty of confidentiality require?

The duty of confidentiality requires that the identity of the whistleblower and other relevant parties (such as persons affiliated with the whistleblower and alleged wrong-doers), or personal data making them identifiable, is not disclosed to anyone beyond people authorized to receive and follow-up whistleblowing reports. This is also known as the 'need-to-know' criteria.

There are limits to confidentiality:

- The identity of the whistleblower can be disclosed if the whistleblower has given explicit consent to do so.
- There can be a legal obligation to disclose the identity in the context of an investigation by national authorities or judicial proceedings.
- In some situations it is likely the identity will be known because it is easy for others to guess who the whistleblower is.

Maintaining confidentiality can be difficult because:

- Personal characteristics or combinations can identify someone (for example voice, accent, gender, small teams or departments, professional affiliations).
- How a whistleblowing report is investigated can unintentionally identify a whistleblower.
- The way outcomes of an investigation or handling process are communicated can identify a whistleblower.

If it is likely that the identity of the whistleblower will be known, or needs to be revealed by law, you should inform the whistleblower before this happens. It is good to consider what additional measures can be taken to protect the whistleblower from harm.

Organizations need to have a plan to deal with breached confidentiality or attempts to identify the whistleblower. This plan will include what additional support can be provided and what disciplinary measures can be taken.

2.1.6 Governance and Training

Normative references include:

- ISO 37002:2021 sections 5.1.1, 5.1.2, 5.2, 5.3.2, 5.3.3, 6.1, 7.3.1, 7.3.2, 7.3.3, 9.1.1, 9.1.2, 10.1
- EU Directive Art. 7.3, 9.1
- EC Expert Group on the Whistleblower Directive letter of 29 June 2021
- ICC section 'Roles and responsibilities', 'Awareness and communication'

Can responsibilities be outsourced?

The EU wants every legal entity of at least 50 workers to develop a capacity for handling whistleblowing reports.

Organizations of less than 250 workers can share resources for whistleblowing channels and investigations. However, they remain responsible for maintaining confidentiality, providing feedback, and addressing the wrongdoing. So, yes, you can hire third-party services to help you meet your obligations, but they remain your obligations.

In line with this, organizations that comprise of several local entities must develop such a capacity at local level. That does not mean there can be no group level centralization at all. It is best to proceed following these three principles: (1) give whistleblowers choice, (2) advocate impartiality, and (3) endorse effective whistleblowing.

Practically speaking:

- Operate at least one channel at local entity level, and one at group level. Clearly indicate this to whistleblowers and let them choose.
- Set out rules for central handling of whistleblowing reports, namely when the reported wrongdoing entails a structural problem exceeding that of the local entity. Communicate these rules in training and whistleblower feedback.
- Inform the whistleblower when invoking these rules and remind them of their option to report the wrongdoing to a national competent authority.
- For organizational monitoring and learning, local entities have to provide group level with case data from which personal data is deleted.

What does the handling function involve?

Every organization has to create an internal function for handling whistleblowing reports and maintaining communication with the whistleblower. One or more persons can be appointed to fulfil this function. If a person fulfils the whistleblowing handling function in addition to other responsibilities, any conflict of interest needs to be avoided.

Check that the handling function:

- Has a mandate that allows impartiality in triage and investigation decisions.
- Has direct and unrestricted access to the different leadership levels of the organization (to top management and board of directors, at local and group level).

What is the role of leadership?

Leadership at all levels of the organization needs to support whistleblowing channels and the handling of whistleblowing reports. This includes management at local and group levels, and also top management and board of directors (or another type of governing body, e.g., in the public sector). In medium sized organizations this might be the same group of people.

Leadership should approve documented information on:

- Decision-making processes to follow-up on whistleblowing reports, including feedback, investigations, protection, sanctions, corrective actions, training, and who will inform authorities when required.
- Evaluate and improve the whistleblowing channels and handling process (who to involve and when to take place).
- Protection measures.
- Data management and confidentiality.

Leadership support at executive and oversight levels means leaders take action with regard to the whistleblowing channels and the handling process, including:

- Repeatedly show their commitment.
- Allocate adequate resources.
- Review operational information.
- Exercise oversight of the impartiality and effectiveness of investigations, protection, and corrective actions.

How can the whistleblowing channel be improved?

To improve the whistleblowing channel, you must first evaluate it. To do that you need to decide:

- What will be monitored and measured? For example: time to close, substantiation rates, anonymous reports, feedback frequency, triage indicators, proactive protection, missed wrongdoing, outcomes for whistleblowers, outcomes for wrongdoers.
- Who will monitor, and when?

- Who will make the evaluation, and when?

An evaluation involves determining the need for change. For example:

- Scope and modalities of whistleblowing channels
- Allocation of resources
- Mandates and responsibilities
- Communication and training
- Data management and confidentiality provisions.

Leadership makes the improvements if it commits to changes determined by the evaluation.

What distinguishes good training?

Training is needed for workers and managers. A good approach is to train people to be in the positions of (1) a potential whistleblower, (2) an alleged wrongdoer, (3) a leadership position.

Check your training covers, at a minimum:

- How a whistleblowing report is handled (because not knowing what happens after a report makes someone lose trust).
- What someone can expect after they made a whistleblowing report (feedback sequence, possible outcomes).
- Protection and confidentiality measures, their limitations and what the whistleblower do.
- Information on:
  - Where a whistleblower can get advice.
  - What the applicable national and EU legislation on whistleblowing and data protection is, and where to find it.
  - What the national competent authority is, and where to locate it.

2.2 Current SUSA Practice

SUSA stands for Speak-Up Self-Assessment. SUSA is a free, online, and anonymous tool that integrity professionals in organizations can use to self-assess how well their internal whistleblowing systems align with the ICC guidance, the ISO37002:2021 standard, and the requirements of the EU Directive 2019/1937.

I developed SUSA as part of the EU-funded BRIGHT project (EACEA101143234). SUSA remains alive and updated thanks to an evolving partnership between EDHEC Business School and Wislport Compliance. We are open to other partnerships in order to keep SUSA running as the free, online, and anonymous tool it was designed to be. Check the SUSA tool to see who the current partners are.

Using SUSA is easy. You can access using the url www.tinyurl.com/edhec-SUSA or a QR code you might find on a flyer or slide when we do a presentation. There is no login required, and we do not store IP address or geolocation data. You will see logos of the current SUSA partners and some available downloads. There is also a link to let us know if you would like to be involved in further research. And of course, you can always go straight to the tool itself. We regularly update SUSA with specific features.

You will see that SUSA is compiled of the different dimensions of a whistleblowing management system, and there are also dimensions relating to organizational culture and a return-value estimate. You can opt to just do one or more specific dimensions. Doing a full SUSA assessment will take you about 45 min. Remember, you are self-assessing, so it is your view on various aspects that is getting assessed. You get an instant calculation of your scoring for every dimension you self-assess. The scoring is as true as what you indicate is going on in your organization. You also see how your scores aggregate into an overall alignment with the ISO37002:2021 standard and the requirements in the EU Whistleblowing Directive. What you will also find on the dashboard is how your scores compare to the SUSA benchmark for each dimension, which is the median score of previous SUSA users.

My advice for using these scores is to see what your current strengths and weaknesses are. The dimensions you score lowest on are likely the aspects you can most easily improve on. You can initially look to the guidance in the first part of this chapter to get ideas for improving your whistleblowing system. This guidance comes with references to the ISO standard, the ICC guidance, and the EU Directive. You can find further inspiration there. You can also work with an external advisor to interpret your SUSA self-assessment to identify ways to improve your whistleblowing system.

SUSA was launched in September 2024. Over the course of just 12 months, by the end of August 2025, SUSA had been used 445 times. The tool provides a lot of flexibility as to how much of it is used. Many users only self-assess a small part. What I did at the end of August 2025, is to take the SUSA data for those who completed 90% or more of the self-assessment tool, and analyze that data. I present some findings here in this chapter.

2.2.1 The SUSA Sample

In the sense of the previous paragraph, the sample used here has n = 126, which gives a response rate of 28.3%. However, there is no way to indicate how representative the sample is. A further limitation is that the SUSA data is fully self-reported without any checks or data entry from outside of SUSA. I present some cross-tabs and correlations in what follows, but these are prone to common method bias. On the other hand, given that SUSA is fully anonymous, there might less tendency for socially desirable responses. In other words, the sample has limitations but respondents might have been more open than in an identified or confidential survey. Nevertheless, it is important to bear in mind that SUSA was designed to help integrity professionals improve their whistleblowing systems, and not as a research tool. A full set of data output is available on: https://doi.org/10.17605/OSF.IO/JSW3Q.

Tables 2.1, 2.2, and 2.3 give an idea of the sample composition. Rounding off percentages, we can see that (Table 2.1) 38.9% of organizations in the sample operate in just one country in the EU, and 11.9% in more than one EU country. There were 29.4% of organizations that operate both within and outside of the EU, and a further 19.8% operate fully outside the EU. We can also see that (Table 2.2) a bit more than 29.4% are public sector organizations (either government agency or government funded), and a bit more than 48% are private sector companies (either publicly traded or privately held). The rest of the sample consists of state-owned enterprises (nearly 9%) and non-profits (a bit more than 13%).

SUSA users tend to come from big organizations (Table 2.3), with 35.8% working in an organization of 5000 or more workers, and 22% in an organization that has between 1000 and 5000 workers. The other size categories are comparable, around

Table 2.1 SUSA sample by countries organizations operate in

	n	%
One country in the EU	49	38.9
More than one country in the EU	15	11.9
Countries both in and out of the EU	37	29.4
One country outside of the EU	12	9.5
More than one country outside of the EU	13	10.3
Total	126	100.0

Table 2.2 SUSA sample by type of organization

	n	%
Government agency	23	18.3
Public sector	14	11.1
State-owned enterprise	11	8.7
For-profit privately held company	32	25.4
For-profit publicly traded company	29	23.0
Private non-profit organization	17	13.5
Total	126	100.0

Table 2.3 SUSA sample by organization size

	n	%
Between 1 and 49	16	13.0
Between 50 and 249	17	13.8
Between 250 and 999	19	15.4
Between 1000 and 4999	27	22.0
5000 or more	44	35.8
Total	123	100.0

15% and 13%. The top five industries are finance/insurance (16%), professional/technical services (12%), health care/social assistance (10%), manufacturing (9%), and transportation/warehousing (7%).

2.2.2 *Channels, Feedback, and Data Management*

The EU Whistleblowing Directive (2019/1937) stipulates that organizations must have channels and a dedicated function to handle reports made through those channels. A further section digs a bit deeper into how that handling function is resourced. Here, I focus on what channels are available, feedback times, and data management provisions of the handling process.

Organizations promote a variety of channels, but there is a clear demarcation. Three types of channels jump out: email (79.7%), in-person meeting (79.5%), and online web-portal (77%). The telephone hotline is promoted by 62% of organizations, and 40% use an organizational ombudsperson or integrity advisor. Only 22% promote a mobile app as whistleblowing channel.

There is broad access to these channels. In nearly 85% of organizations in the sample, the reporting channels can be used by all workers in the organization regardless of their type of contract (Table 2.4). The trend is less clear when it comes to what kind of wrongdoing or concerns can be reported through those channels (see Table 2.5). In the SUSA sample, 15.2% remain overly narrow by only accepting legal breaches, and 29.6% limit the material scope to code of conduct breaches. Slightly half of organizations are more relaxed about what can be reported through the channels: 34.4% has opened the channels for any concern except personal matters, and 20.8% does not impose any limitation.

Feedback to those who report through the channels, however, is not good (Table 2.6). Almost one in five does not provide an initial acknowledgment to the whistleblower that their report was received, or does not know whether or when that

Table 2.4 Stakeholder access to the organizational whistleblowing channels

	n	%
Workers from a specific department	3	2.4
All workers with an employment contract from the organization	13	10.4
All workers in the organization (directly employed, agency workers, interns, etc.)	31	24.8
Every worker in the supply chain (workers in the organization, in the subcontractors, and in the client organizations)	18	14.4
Everyone (workers, clients, customers, the public)	57	45.6
Don't know	3	2.4
Total	125	100.0

Table 2.5 Material scope of organizational whistleblowing channels

	n	%
Legal breaches only	19	15.2
All code of conduct breaches	37	29.6
Any concern (except personal matters)	43	34.4
Really any concern	26	20.8
Total	125	100.0

happens. Only 55.2% complies with the EU requirement of providing such acknowledgment of receipt within seven days. Further feedback to the whistleblower about how their report is handled also shows a very low compliance rate (Table 2.7). Only 44.1% comply with the EU requirement of providing such further feedback within three months of receiving the report. A further 44.9% provides such feedback at the end of the process, whenever that is.

Data management of reports during the handling process is obviously very important for effective and trustworthy whistleblowing systems. The EU Directive (2019/1937) is quite explicit in Art.17 that the EU Regulation 2016/679, also known as GDPR, applies to personal data processed pursuant to the Whistleblowing Directive. The SUSA data suggests organizations are missing quite some checks there.

Only 65% of the SUSA sample was able to acknowledge that there is a list of mandate holders for dealing with cases. Of those, 89% said the list was up-to-date, 77% said the list was adaptable per case to avoid conflict of interest, and 84% said the list was adaptable if needed in order to maintain confidentiality. Data management was further of poor quality when we look at specific requirements of the GDPR

Table 2.6 Initial acknowledgment of receipt given to whistleblower in less than seven days

	n	%
Always	69	55.2
Most of the time	20	16.0
Sometimes	12	9.6
Never	2	1.6
Don't know	22	17.6
Total	125	100.0

Table 2.7 Feedback beyond the initial acknowledgment

	n	%
Within three months	52	44.1
Only at the end of the process, whenever that is	53	44.9
No further feedback is given	13	11.0
Total	118	100.0

Table 2.8 Data management provisions for handling whistleblowing reports (n = 115)

Data management policy includes the following with regard to whistleblowing:	*n*	%
Instructions for retention and disposition of data during the handling of a case	67	58.3
Instructions for retention and disposition of data after the handling of a case	69	60.0
Instructions for avoiding the collecting of personal data that is not relevant	55	47.8
Instructions for modification of personal identifiable information	51	44.3
Instructions for deleting accidentally collected irrelevant personal data	48	41.7
Giving notice regarding collected data	48	41.7

(Table 2.8). The item that scores best is that the data management policy includes instructions for retention of data after the handling of a whistleblowing case, but that is only 60%. Data management policies do not seem to consider that whistleblowing reports are bound to include personal data, and that it is therefore necessary to include instructions for modification of such data (44.3%), or deleting accidentally collected irrelevant personal data (41.7%). Giving notice to whistleblowers of what personal data is collected and for what purposes, also remains a poorly practiced requirement (41.7%).

2.2.3 *Protection*

Only 67% of organizations in the SUSA sample had the responsibility for protection and support of the whistleblower clearly assigned to someone within the organization. That does not imply the function performs well in two out of three organizations. Some indication of unclear roles here are that only 49% indicates that protection measures are discussed with the whistleblower, and a mere 39% says they review protection measures after some time together with the whistleblower. I discuss these findings further in chapter three.

Organizational measures to remedy harm to whistleblowers tend to be ad hoc and improvised, indications that organizations are not well equipped to protect their whistleblowers (Table 2.9). An item in SUSA relates to whether the organization has clear and document processes in place in case a whistleblower experiences harm in relation to making a report. Only 51.2% said they had this for reinstating the whistleblower in the same or equivalent position (e.g., salary, position, responsibilities). That is low but for other remedies this falls even below the ‘pure luck’ benchmark. Only 48.8% have documented remedy processes for providing fair access to benefits and entitlements, only 46.3% for providing fair access to promotion, and also 45.8%

Table 2.9 Organizations that have clear and documented processes for remedy of whistleblower harm (n = 121)

If the whistleblower experiences harm in relation to making a report, the organization has clear and documented processes in place to offer the whistleblower the following:	*n*	%
Reinstating in the same or equivalent position (e.g., salary, position, responsibilities)	62	51.2
Provide fair access to benefits and entitlements	59	48.8
Provide fair access to promotion	56	46.3
Provide fair access to training and opportunities55	55	45.8
Giving apologies	45	37.2
Withdrawal of litigation	38	31.4
Compensating for damage	33	27.3

for providing fair access to training and opportunities. Only 37.2% had a documented process for giving apologies to whistleblowers, and 31.4% for withdrawal of litigation against whistleblowers. Only 27.3% said they have a documented process for compensating damage to a whistleblower.

2.2.4 *Governance*

Although organizations of up to 249 workers can share resources to handle internal whistleblowing reports, the initial idea of the Expert Group (cf. its letter from 29 June 2021) was that every legal entity was required to develop capacity to handle reports. The implication was that big corporate groups could not centralize resources to concentrate the report handling and whistleblower support at group level only. This was a surprising position, given that it seems plausible to assume that well-resourced dedicated teams would be able to handle reports in a more impartial manner, but that small organization might not be able to appropriately resource and mandate such a team. This section provides some analysis of the SUSA data that sheds light on that assumption.

There is support for the hypothesis that bigger organizations will be able to allocate more time to the whistleblowing handling function. Non-parametric Spearman's rho test was used to see whether the number of people working in an organization correlated with the time allocated in the organization to the function for day-to-day management of the whistleblowing procedures, i.e., the whistleblowing function. This gave a significant correlation ($p < .01$) of close to moderate strength ($rho = .271$).

However, the size of an organization did not have statistically significant associations with other indicators of quality governance. We tested the associations with variables relating to the whistleblowing officer, i.e., the function that is responsible for day-to-day management of the whistleblowing procedures. We tested these as nominal by nominal, using the non-parametric Cramer's V test. The tests did not provide grounds to see an association between number of workers in the organization and a range of outsourcing decisions. Nor did size of the organization associate with how well the whistleblowing function was resourced, how good the decision-making authority was, whether the whistleblowing function has direct access to the board, or whether the persons in that role were representative of the diversity in the organization. Size did have some association with type of organization ($p < .05$) at moderate association (.275), but type of organization did not associate with any of the governance indicators.

Further tests did reveal that governance indicators are associated, but not with size of the organization. We visualize these in Fig. 2.1. I only include moderate and strong associations. A couple of observations are noteworthy here. The first is that there is a salient triangle of association between seeing the whistleblowing function well resourced, direct access of that function to the board, and strong mandate of the whistleblowing function (i.e., decision-making autonomy). The strongest associations are between these three variables. The second point is that both the resourcing as well as the mandate of the whistleblowing function show some association with how much time is allocated to that function. This suggests that the perception of the quality and strength of the whistleblowing function implies that it has some presence within the organization, and that it cannot be fully outsourced. To put it more succinctly, it seems that the perception of a strong mandate is an internal mandate. A third observation is that well-resourced and strongly mandated whistleblowing functions show an association with representing the workforce in terms of personal protected characteristics, such as gender. On the one hand, it should not be surprising that DEI representativeness of the whistleblowing function is among the indicators that can signal governance quality of a whistleblowing system. On the other hand, it is surprising that no association was found between DEI representativeness of and time allocated to the whistleblowing function. This mixed finding is, I believe, sufficient reason for qualitative and case study research into DEI aspects of whistleblowing functions in organizations. Further indicators and frameworks for such research have been developed as part of the BRIGHT project and are available open access (see Kenny & Milàn, 2025).

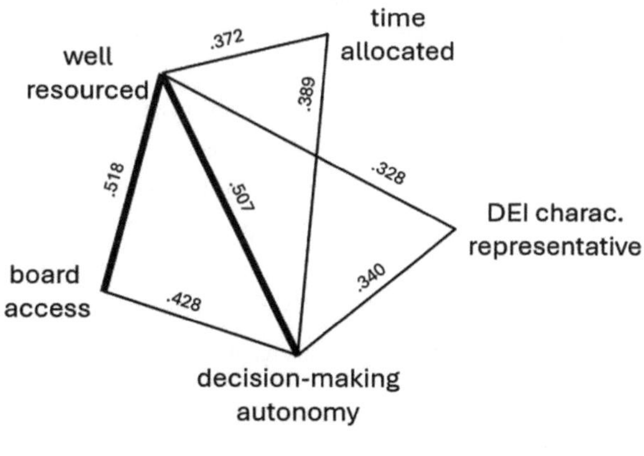

Fig. 2.1 Moderate and strong associations between SUSA governance indicators ($n = 124$, Cramer's V, all $p < .001$)

2.2.5 Cultures

The SUSA tool includes measures for organizational culture based on two validated scales (Edmondson, 1999; Kaptein, 2008). The SUSA tool asks for perception mainly about work floor level culture using items from the psychological safety scale (Edmondson, 1999), and middle level management culture using items from the discussability scale (Kaptein, 2008). In a further analysis presented here, a measure was calculated for top level culture. As a proxy for this, the items asking whether top management and governing body support the whistleblowing policy in external and internal communication were used.

The analysis did not find grounds to see an association between type of organization and how the SUSA user perceives work floor culture or top management culture. The association with middle management culture is more interesting. I provide a summary of the findings for that in Table 2.10.

The statistical significance is just outside the 95% confidence level, at.051. The strength of association is moderate (.436). Table 2.10 shows, per type of organization, the percentage of organizations that had a culture perception score at the low (2 or less) and the high ends (6 or more). Three groups can be discerned in the sample. State-owned enterprises and non-profit organizations had none in the low scores and most in the high scores, respectively 60% and 40%. The second group is comprised of government agencies and private held for-profit organizations. These had both a U-shaped scoring, although skewed toward the higher scores. The third group is the public sector organizations and the publicly traded organizations. They had the least high scoring organizations. It is difficult to theorize explanations for this fuzzy grouping.

Table 2.11 provides some further insights in the perceptions of cultures in organizations. The more SUSA users perceive the whistleblowing function to have high decision-making autonomy, the better they perceive cultures at all three levels: top, middle management, and work floor. The correlation of the decision-making autonomy of the whistleblowing function with perception of middle management

Table 2.10 Type of organization and perception of management culture (%)

Score management culture 2-or-less	Type of organization	Score management culture 6-or more
16.8	Government agency	31.6
7.1	Public sector	14.2
0.0	State-owned enterprise	60.0
14.8	For-profit privately held	29.6
0.0	For-profit publicly traded	21.4
0.0	Not-for profit private	40.0

$p = .051$; Cramer's V association strength.436, $df = 85$

Table 2.11 Correlations between decision-making autonomy of whistleblowing function and perceptions of culture at different levels (non-parametric Spearman rho)

	Decision-making autonomy	Perception of work floor culture	Perception of management culture	Perception of top culture
Decision-making autonomy	1000			
Perception of work floor culture	.439**	1000		
Perception of management culture	.564**	.653**	1000	
Perception of top culture	.247**	.157	.227*	1000

** Correlation is significant at the 0.01 level (2-tailed)
* Correlation is significant at the 0.05 level (2-tailed)

culture is strong (.564), with work floor culture moderate (.439), and a weak correlation was found with perception of top management culture (.247). Of course, the limitation to the generalizability of the findings and its implications stems from the way the measures for culture as well as that for function autonomy were arrived at. These are self-reported individual perceptions.

Despite these limitations, these findings support the assertion that the role of the whistleblowing function can be a builder of organizational culture, but more so at lower and middle levels in the organization than at top level. In the next chapter, I delve into that. I present research into how people in a whistleblowing function or related roles are trying to build organizational culture by making the internal whistleblowing systems trustworthy.

References

Del Monte, M., & Faucheux, T. (2024). *Protecting whistle-blowers in the EU. Briefing*. European Parliamentary Research Service. Retrieved October 9, 2025, from https://www.europarl.europa.eu/RegData/etudes/BRIE/2023/747103/EPRS_BRI(2023)747103_EN.pdf

Edmondson, A. (1999). Psychological safety and learning behavior in work teams. *Administrative Science Quarterly, 44*(2), 350–383.

Kaptein, M. (2008). Developing and testing a measure for the ethical culture of organizations: The corporate ethical virtues model. *Journal of Organizational Behavior, 29*(7), 923–947.

Kenny, K., & Milán, T. (2025). *Gender and intersectionality mainstreaming in whistleblowing systems (GIM-Tool)*. University of Galway. Retrieved October 9, 2025, from https://doi.org/10.13025/29814

Vandekerckhove, W. (2022). Is it freedom? The coming about of the EU directive on whistleblower protection. *Journal of Business Ethics, 179*(1), 1–11.

Wim Vandekerckhove is (Full) Professor of Business Ethics at EDHEC Business School in France. He holds a PhD from Ghent University. Before joining EDHEC, he has held academic affiliations to Ghent University (Belgium), the University of Oslo (Norway), Griffith University (Australia), the International Anti-Corruption Academy (Austria), and the University of Greenwich (UK). Wim has been Editor-in-Chief for *Philosophy of Management*, and is currently Consulting Editor for the *Journal of Business Ethics*. Wim has provided expertise to various organizations, including Council of Europe, United Nations Office on Drugs and Crime (UNODC), the International Olympic Committee (IOC), Transparency International, the UK Department of Health, the UK Financial Conduct Authority. He is a committee member of the British Standards Institute (BSI) on governance. He led the development of ISO37002:2021, the international standard for Whistleblowing Management Systems, and participated in developing BS25700 Organizational Responses to Modern Slavery.

Chapter 3
Benefits of Internal Channels for Building Cultures of Trust

Abstract This chapter suggests how formal internal whistleblowing channels and handling processes can support building informal cultures of trust in organizations. It starts by using SUSA data to show where organizations leave opportunities untapped to create more trustworthy whistleblowing systems and cultures of trust. The research suggests PDCA cycles for continuous improvement are not fully implemented. The chapter then proceeds to analyze why integrity professionals tend to struggle making the organizational whistleblowing channels trustworthy. This analysis relies on signaling theory and the ABI-model of trustworthiness.

3.1 From Channels to Cultures

In this section I use some insights from SUSA to say something about whistleblowing channels and organizational culture. I draw on some further data from SUSA not yet included in the previous chapter. It is data that shows gaps and a disconnect between a formal box-tick and an engagement to make a whistleblowing system responsive.

The relationship between organizational whistleblowing channels and organizational culture is not evident. Internal channels are formal reporting channels. A culture of trust relates to routines and habits, "the way we do things here", and so is quite informal. An often used definition of organizational culture is that it is the learned and shared assumptions, values, and behaviors of members of an organization. Cabana and Kaptein (2021) make a strong case that culture is best understood at team level rather than at organizational level. An organization usually has more than one culture, depending on what part of the organization you are looking at. Team culture thus 'encompasses the assumptions, values, and behaviors shared by individuals working together on a daily basis within the same suborganizational unit' (Cabana & Kaptein, 2021: 762). SUSA does not capture how people in different teams of an organization do things; rather it measures how one person perceives culture at different levels in the organization: work floor, middle management, and top management. In what follows, I continue to use the term 'organizational culture' but do so for the grouping of cultures in different parts and levels of the organization.

W. Vandekerckhove, *Whistleblowing Management Systems and Speak-Up Cultures*, SpringerBriefs in Business, https://doi.org/10.1007/978-3-032-14204-7_3

The ideal we have of a speak-up culture, which we tend to characterize as a high-trust culture, is that workers will report a doubt or a worry to their direct manager, or openly in a meeting. We know from research that people use an internal whistle-blowing channel when they are afraid of speaking directly with their manager, or they have tried to raise a concern with their manager but got a weird response. In research I did together with Arron Phillips, we traced in over 800 cases how people attempt to raise a concern about wrongdoing in their workplace (Vandekerckhove & Phillips, 2019). We found that whistleblowing is a protracted process rather than a one-off decision. Earlier research (e.g., Rotschild & Miethe, 1999) had indicated that people tended to raise a concern inside their organization before doing so to a regulatory agency or to a journalist. What I found in the research with Phillips was that of those who go on to make four attempts to raise a concern, half still do so internally to their organization. It was a surprise to us to find whistleblowing remains inside the organization so long. This led us to theorize that the protraction of the whistleblowing process is a search for a more impartial recipient at each successive attempt to raise the concern, and people often believe they can find that impartial recipient inside their organization (Vandekerckhove & Phillips, 2019).

In 9 out of 10 cases the person first tried to raise their concern with their direct manager. I write 'tried' because the whistleblowing process starts to protract when an attempt to raise a concern is not heard. We found the most common response that people experienced was being neglected, more so than experiencing retaliation after their first attempt to raise a concern. Only after that would people try to raise their concern with a higher manager or the organization's whistleblowing channel. Hence, in a sense, whistleblowing channels are used when there is a lack of trust in the direct manager. They initially did trust their manager and raised their concern with them, but were ignored or experienced detriment because of it, and now no longer trust their manager. They nevertheless still trust the organization because people overwhelmingly remain inside the organization in their attempts to raise a concern.

This leads me to a first point, namely that formal reporting channels would not be needed in a culture of trust, or a speak-up culture. Psychological safety is an often used construct in organizational behavior that captures some of what is meant with a speak-up culture, I believe. The construct was developed by Amy Edmondson (1999). She defines 'team psychological safety' as 'a shared belief that the team is safe for interpersonal risk taking' (Edmondson, 1999: 354). It is not the same as 'group cohesiveness', which is known to reduce people's willingness to disagree and challenge each other. For Edmondson, team psychological safety goes beyond inter-personal trust and characterizes something people perceive at team level, namely trust and mutual respect 'in which people are comfortable being themselves'. Edmondson (1999) finds it has a positive impact on learning behaviors in organizations as well as people's ability to deal with organizational change.

It is useful to include some of the items from Edmondson's validated scale for measuring team psychological safety into staff surveys. Depending on how people answer, they perceive more or less psychological safety in their workplace. The scale's items also make this construct concrete and easy for us to understand. If you look up the items in the original research paper (see Edmondson, 1999) you will see that some items need to be reverse coded. But if you allow me to approach the scale as an every-day expression of what 'team psychological safety' actually looks like, then I would say that we are perceiving more psychological safety when we find that:

1) If we make a mistake it is not held against us.
2) You notice colleagues talking about problems and difficult issues.
3) People in the team are not rejected because they are different.
4) If you feel it is safe to take a risk openly.
5) If it is easy to ask others for help.
6) There is psychological safety if you feel that no one would deliberately undermine you.
7) And when you feel your skills and talents are valued by those in your team.

So that is where you want to get to really; that is the goal of building a culture of trust. This goal is quite different from operating formal channels through which people can report wrongdoing. Indeed, implementing whistleblowing channels is not the same as building a culture of trust but neither are they opposed to such a culture. Formal channels can help you build that informal culture, but for that to happen you need to manage them as a system. I explain in the remainder of this section what that entails.

I already suggested that when people report to an internal whistleblowing channel, it can be an indication of lack of trust. People report through a formal channel because they do not trust their team members, or because they do not trust their direct manager. However, it is also important to note that when people report through an internal whistleblowing channel, they do trust the organization. Trust works at different levels. People don't trust their manager but they do trust the internal channel is working well, and they trust the organization will handle their report in an impartial way.

Whistleblowers typically raise their concern more than once, most often directly with the wrongdoer or their line manager in the first instance, expecting the person they address to take action to stop the alleged wrongdoing. If this expectation is not met—i.e., the wrongdoing is not addressed or the whistleblower begins to experience reprisals—then they might raise their concern again with someone else, either inside the organization or externally, to a regulator or a journalist, and more rarely the ombudsperson, the trade union or professional body. A decisive factor for internal whistleblowers to escalate their whistleblowing to external recipients such as regulators or the media appears to be the actual or anticipated responses whistleblowers receive when they raise their concerns informally with their line manager.

Hence, the question is not channels versus culture. Rather, the question is how we go from trust in the *organization* to trust *within* the organization. How do we go from channels that work well and a well mandated whistleblowing officer, to psychological safety and trust culture? How do we go from formal interventions to informal capacity? Before going into this, I would like to tell, as an anecdote, the story of how an engineering company built a culture of trust. The full case study is in a book I published with Kate Kenny and Mariana Fotaki (Kenny et al., 2019). The book contains four case studies of organizations doing a great job at implementing internal channels and building cultures of trust. The engineering firm was one of them and illustrates we need to be patient as well as persistent. The company had gone through a huge scandal that had severely affected trust within the company. In response, and partly imposed as a regulatory sanction, the company had restructured and reinforced a central compliance function. They had implemented internal whistleblowing channels and found that more than 7 years later, they had built a culture of trust.

Their seven-year journey looked like this. When they started, they put in place a reporting channel and a question channel. At first, the question channel was used way more than the reporting channel. It is easy to understand why. Trust in the organization is low, as is trust within the teams. The threshold is lower when you're just asking a hypothetical question; you're not accusing anyone. And asking questions also gets you to know where the line is. The compliance team at headquarters were able to answer these questions, and the company was thus seen to be responsive. When people saw that this worked, the company saw the reporting channel being used more often. They had built trust in the organization.

And then they saw the reporting channel frequency go down a bit and settle on a stable number, much lower than its peak. But they heard from their local compliance folks close to the projects and the work floor, that people were directly coming to them more often, making reports in person to them, talking to them. They realized that what had happened was that persistence in making the channels work and improve, had built culture. But it took 7 years. I believe we can achieve this much quicker. We don't need to hope for trust; we can plan and organize to build a culture of trust. When you manage your whistleblowing channels as management systems, you can go from formal interventions to informal capacity.

The EU Whistleblowing Directive (2019/1937) requires organizations to have channels, and to mandate a function—a whistleblowing officer—to handle the reports. Article 9.1(c) stipulates that procedures for internal reporting need to include:

> the designation of an impartial person or department competent for following-up on the reports which may be the same person or department as the one that receives the reports and which will maintain communication with the reporting person and, where necessary, ask for further information from and provide feedback to that reporting person

We are seeing organizations develop that. It is possible that we are seeing better channels, and handling functions with better mandates. It's also possible we are seeing whistleblowing officers with more experience. However, in the organizations I have seen these often remain very lonely roles. On the one hand, their time allocation is improving, as is their mandate, but they are lonely in carrying all the responsibilities for whistleblowing in the organization. And that is a problem.

To explain why that is a problem and what is needed to fix it, I want to look again at the ISO37002:2021 standard. In the previous chapter I explained how this international standard for internal whistleblowing systems came about. The term 'system' is important here because ISO37002:2021 is a management systems standard. This means that the standard is designed in a plan-do-check-act (PDCA) cyclical architecture. The PDCA model is a well-known basis for continuous improvement of processes. It is quite basic as a management technique and hence should be familiar with managers in all kinds of organizations. If you allow me to simplify matters a bit, we could say that the 'Plan' stage for whistleblowing systems is in creating the channels, mandating the roles, communicating the policy, determining scope, and training everyone. My impression is that organizations are getting better at this. The 'Do' stage is the actual handling process of whistleblowing reports. This is the core of the ISO37002:2021, with plenty of guidance on the various steps in the handling process, and how to maintain trust and impartiality. It's possible organizations are getting better at this too, perhaps because these roles are starting to professionalize away from the strictly legal or human resources profiles.

So, what we have is that organizations are getting better at planning the handling process and the mandate of the whistleblowing officer function. It means channels do work better. But it is isolated and still not building culture. Because although they get better at Plan—Do, they are still neglecting Check—Act. The 'Check' stage is the evaluation of the whistleblowing system, and the 'Act' stage is making changes to the system based on the evaluation. It is in the Check—Act part that the opportunity lies to get other functions within the organization some ownership of how the organization responds to people reporting wrongdoing, and people raising concerns.

The ISO37002:2021 standard sees this opportunity when you take a step back—once a year or so—to look what the system has done. Questions you need to ask include:

- What was reported? What bad stuff happened but wasn't reported?
- What are the experiences of those who used the channels?
- What were the difficulties in handling those reports and protecting our whistleblowers?

You have to reflect on that with different functions of the organization and decide who needs to act and change approach. This is one important way in which you can go from formal channels to informal culture of trust. Break the isolation of the whistleblowing officer function and create a wider ownership of the culture. But organizations are not doing this enough. Let me illustrate this with some SUSA findings.

There are two findings from SUSA that I want to show here. Both relate to approaching your channels as a management system. And both indicate organizations are not doing this enough. The first is about whistleblower protection. In the SUSA sample, 66.9% of organizations have a dedicated function for that. That is not bad, but what do they do? Table 3.1 lists some items that pertain to the organizational capacity to protect its whistleblowers.

Only 60% does pro-active assessment of retaliation risk; the rest waits until it goes wrong. Only 52% has a documented set of protection measures, ready to be used when needed. It gets worse. Only 49.2% discusses protection measures with the whistleblower, and a mere 39.5% reviews these together with the whistleblower. 40.8% takes particular vulnerabilities into account. So, the situation is as follows. Most organizations have someone who can make decisions on protecting employees who report wrongdoing. But these protections are ad hoc, not discussed with those who get the protection, and not reviewed with them after a period of time. The picture

Table 3.1 Protection capacity for whistleblowers in organizations ($n = 126$)

SUSA participants who said 'yes' to the following questions:	*n*	%
Is responsibility for protection and support of the whistleblower clearly assigned to someone within the organization?	83	66.9
Does triage include a risk assessment of possible whistleblower retaliation?	75	60.0
Is there a range of clearly described and actionable protection measures?	64	52.0
Does assessment of which groups of workers are particularly vulnerable to reprisal in your organization form part of protection measures?	51	40.8
Are protection measures always discussed with the whistleblower?	61	49.2
Are protection measures reviewed after some time together with the whistleblower?	49	39.5

is one where we're protecting someone, without telling them and without asking them how it goes. We must be ticking a box somewhere but we're definitely not building culture here.

The second finding relates to the evaluation of the system. It gives an indication of how unsystematic the approach is. Of the organizations in the SUSA sample, 50.9% have a documented process for evaluating the whistleblowing system. That is quite low. Table 3.2 shows what the indicators are for evaluating whistleblowing systems. Or rather, what indicators are not used. The best scoring indicator is the time taken to acknowledge receipt of the report. Other indicators are used by less than 40% of organizations.

Many times, no one checks whether a corrective action actually stopped the wrongdoing or whether sanctions have worked. Only a minority are interested in getting some feedback from those who used the channels, in order to improve the channels. Only a third measures how people in the organization perceive the reporting channels and whether they even know where to find them. This is a nightmare in terms of quality management and it sure doesn't build culture.

The point I want to make here is that breaking the isolation of the handling function—the whistleblowing officer—is necessary for building a culture of trust.

Table 3.2 Indicators for evaluating whistleblowing systems ($n = 126$)

SUSA participants who respond 'yes' to the question whether the following indicators are used when evaluating the whistleblowing system:	*n*	%
Time taken to acknowledge receipt	57	45.2
Time taken for each step in handling process	43	34.1
Feedback from whistleblower about handling process	48	38.1
Periodic survey of workers about awareness and trust in channels	41	32.5
Proportion of reports resulting in corrective actions	44	34.9
Effectiveness of corrective actions	40	31.7
Information about whistleblower retaliation	43	34.1
Employment outcomes for whistleblowers	39	31.0

But does that mean all team managers, at all levels, need to know how to handle reports of wrongdoing? Do they all need to be able to make protection decisions? What kind of mandate would that require? And is that not too much weight on their shoulders? I would like to suggest a possible way to resolve this tension, a suggestion of how you can build that culture in a realistic way.

For that, I want to draw your attention to another validated scale to measure a construct, this time by Muel Kaptein. Kaptein (2008) developed the CEV model—Corporate Ethical Virtues. There are 7 virtues, or seven characteristics and organization must have for it to have an ethical culture. One of these is discussability. With this corporate virtue, Kaptein eyes the opposite of moral disengagement, when people 'figuratively close their ears and eyes to what they do not want to hear or see' (Kaptein, 2008: 926). Instead, people need to be given broad scope to exchange, analyze, and discuss their experiences, including near-misses, transgressions, and dilemmas. Kaptein (2008: 927) further posits that 'if moral issues are not openly spoken about, they go unnoticed and unacknowledged, which leads to higher moral stress and a decline of moral authority of normative expectations'. Table 3.3 lists the 10 items that make up the scale to measure 'discussability'. These items—or some of them—can be used in a staff survey to get a measure that can help in seeing differences across the organization or across time.

My point with showing this, is that for a culture of trust we need people to feel comfortable in pointing out things that go wrong, by talking about it and reporting it. And that is discussability. Again, items in a validated scale to measure this construct give us an idea of what discussability looks like in an every-day work context. What I want to suggest however, is that in Kaptein's items, we can distinguish two different levels. Hence, when it comes to who needs to do what, not every team manager needs to have the expertise or mandate of the whistleblowing officer who handles the formal reports.

What a line manager at team level needs to accomplish is that:

- People in their team have an opportunity to express their opinion
- That time is available during meetings to discuss what ethical conduct is

Table 3.3 Kaptein's 10 items of the discussability scale (amended from Kaptein, 2008)

1. Reports of unethical conduct are handled with caution
2. I have the opportunity to express my opinion
3. There is adequate scope to discuss ethical conduct
4. Reports of unethical conduct are taken seriously
5. There is adequate scope to discuss personal moral dilemmas
6. There is adequate scope to report unethical conduct
7. There is ample opportunity for discussing moral dilemmas
8. If someone is called to account for his/her conduct, it is done in a respectful manner
9. There is adequate scope to correct unethical conduct
10. There is sufficient opportunity to raise the matter elsewhere in the organization

- And it is both acceptable and there is time to discuss personal moral dilemmas
- And then also, when someone does something wrong, they are called to account in a respectful manner

This set of items is at the team level; every manager needs to make this happen in their team. The whistleblowing officer then, does the other things that make up discussability:

- Ensure impartiality when handling reports
- Follows a process that ensures reports are taken seriously
- A broad range of issues can be reported and triaged
- Investigations will be followed-up with corrective action
- Everyone knows they can use the channel if they cannot speak up in their teams

Conceiving a division of labor between levels in an organization is a way to leverage trust in the organization to create trust within the organization. In this section I also suggested that internal channels and a mandated whistleblowing officer can build a culture of trust and psychological safety, but only if the whistleblowing system is managed as a full Plan-Do-Check-Act cycle. The move from formal channels to informal culture requires breaking the isolation of the formal channels and the whistleblowing officer, and get broad shoulders throughout the organization to carry the culture of trust.

In the next section, I look closer at the loneliness of integrity professionals who try to make the organizational whistleblowing channels trustworthy. They are confronted with different expectations and often struggle to adequately make sense of what signals they are sending to their internal stakeholders, i.e., workers, middle managers, and top management.

3.2 Making Channels Trustworthy

This section explores how organizational actors attempt to make internal whistleblowing systems trustworthy for their stakeholders (whistleblowing employees, alleged wrongdoers, line managers, and top management). It is based on a larger research project I did with colleagues at various institutions outside EDHEC: Marianna Fotaki, Kate Kenny, and Didem Derya Özdemir Kaya (see Vandekerckhove et al., 2025). Examining trustworthiness in the context of whistleblowing channels is vital for understanding their effectiveness. Hardin (2002) pointed out that although we speak of trust, it is really trustworthiness we are after. Although the concepts are related, trustworthiness is not the same as trust. Rather, trustworthiness is the antecedent of trust. The former indicates a belief in the potential recipient of trust (trustee), and the latter is an action by an actor who trusts (trustor). Put differently, trustworthiness is a quality that the trustee is perceived to have while trusting is something that the trustor does. As individuals become more dependent on, and more vulnerable to, the decisions and actions of others, trust is increasingly seen as an organizing principle influencing interaction patterns and organizational processes (McEvily et al., 2003). Though there is no single definition of trust because it differs according to discipline and context, there is wide agreement that trusting behaviors arise out of the need to decrease uncertainty and minimize the risk of unpredictable consequences of actions by others on whom we depend. This leads to positive expectations (Rousseau et al., 1998) and the suspension of disbelief but requires a 'leap of faith' (Möllering, 2006).

Trustworthiness is a state we must signal to create belief. This is crucial when operating internal whistleblowing arrangements since this implies maintaining organizational trust, despite a lack of trust at the individual level between employee and line manager, throughout a sequence of interactions involving multiple trustors: the stakeholders trusting the existing arrangements and those who operate them (trustees). The lack of trust occurs because whistleblowing or reporting internally happens at a point when the individual witnessed wrongdoing, might have sought help to address the wrongdoing and was ignored. This chapter draws on findings from a qualitative study (Vandekerckhove et al., 2025) with people operating internal whistleblowing systems in four organizations: a hospital in the UK, an engineering multinational, a bank with offices in Western Europe and the US, and a central government agency in Southeast Asia. These were very different organizations, and the individuals overseeing and running the internal whistleblowing channels in those organizations, had very different functions. We started using the term Internal Whistleblowing Recipients (IWRs) for all of these functions that had an operational or coordinating role. In the bigger research project, we were looking for cases where the implementation of whistleblowing systems seemed to work well. We published on these four case studies elsewhere (Kenny et al., 2019).

What we noticed was that the IWRs were putting a lot of effort into trying to be trustworthy. They tried to signal the trustworthiness of the channels and the handling process to different internal stakeholders—whistleblowers, middle and top managers. This also seemed to imply that they themselves had to be seen as trustworthy professionals. Apparently, this was not obvious. Being trustworthy to those different internal stakeholders, and maintaining their trust, was something they worried about. We found this very intriguing and decided to dig a bit deeper to explore how we could understand and explain those worries. We ended up drawing on the ABI-model of trustworthiness attributions developed by Mayer et al. (1995) and expanded by Pirson and Malhotra (2011).

The starting point is that trust in a supervisor substantially influences employees' trust in their senior management more generally (Kannan-Narasimhan & Lawrence, 2012). However, when initial attempts to raise a concern with the line manager fail, another option for the whistleblower is to report to the organization, through the internal whistleblowing system. Retaining a potential whistleblower's trust in internal channels can prove difficult. Critical to an organization's success in encouraging internal speak-up, and dealing with wrongdoing, is the provision of an adequate whistleblowing system, meaning fit for purpose, impartial, and crucially, effective in stopping the wrongdoing. Waiting for decisions, non-forthcoming decisions (because of limitations on what can be communicated), delayed decisions, can also affect the trustworthiness of organizational processes and those who operate these. Organizations may compete with regulators for the whistleblower's information, with trustworthiness being an essential currency in this struggle. In that sense, signaling trustworthiness in the internal whistleblowing channels by the Internal Whistleblowing Recipient (IWR) could prevent the whistleblower from turning away from the organization after they lost trust in their line manager.

However, we saw IWRs facing different expectations from their internal stakeholders, and we saw them struggling to cope with those expectations. We thus realized that establishing trust in the internal whistleblowing system means that the IWRs need to convince each stakeholder of trustworthiness attributions specific to the respective stakeholders. As Hardin (2002, p. 34) wrote: 'Making oneself trustworthy is convincing the trustor of one's commitment to fulfil the trustor's trust'. Our research was able to shed light on how IWRs seek to do this, and what difficulties they face.

The well-known ABI-model developed by Mayer et al. (1995), distinguishes three dimensions of trustworthiness: 1) Ability: the trustor believes the trustee has the required competence to do what the trustor trusts them to do; 2) Benevolence: the trustor believes the trustee has good intentions and will not take advantage and will be concerned for the trustor's well-being; 3) Integrity: the trustor believes the trustee acts according to a set of principles that the trustor finds acceptable. Pirson and Malhotra (2011) added transparency as a separate dimension: 4) Transparency: the trustor believes the trustee is willing to share trust-relevant information with the trustor.

For the methodological aspects of the research, how we collected and analyzed the data, I refer to Vandekerckhove et al. (2025). Here, I want to revisit a selection of the findings to bring out some insights relevant to this book, which is about building culture from channels.

3.2.1 Signaling Trustworthiness

The data from the research (Vandekerckhove et al., 2025) includes many instances where IWRs indicated various ways in which they tried to signal trustworthiness to whistleblowing employees and other internal stakeholders like line managers and the top management. I show a selection here using the trustworthiness attributes discussed in the previous section: ability, benevolence, integrity, and transparency. Instance of IWRs signaling ability were mainly to two trustors: whistleblowers and the top management. For example, in the bank, the speak-up system was promoted as part of the policy portfolio:

> So, the policies are very publicized on the intranet and regularly we would send out updates or draw people's attention to it. And we also have e-learning and training in relation to various policies and procedures. And that would reference various different mechanisms for staff members to address any of the issues that they might have. (Esther, HR manager, bank)

The bank's speak-up system was one of the 'mechanisms' that enabled the organization to be responsive to 'staff members' issues. Through training, the IWRs were telling potential whistleblowers how they—and thus the organization—could hear them. To top management, however, ability-signaling by IWRs consisted of having data:

> I can tell you immediately how many cases we have in this division, and in that division, or in a corporate call unit. I can tell you in what country we have how many cases, and I can tell you which channel they come from. (Hannah, HR Lead for speak-up, engineering)

Here, the IWR explains how possessing this information puts them in a position of control, with oversight of the situation, while offering reassurance to top management. On the other hand, the signaling of benevolence by IWR seemed most easily done towards whistleblowers, as the following quotes illustrate:

> The protection of the identity is very important for a reporter, meaning that his identity is not disclosed to either the compliance organization or the company in general, and this forms part of the very first information given to the reporter. (Peter, Head of Compliance, engineering)

> It's the confidential question again of, "Yes, your details will remain here. It doesn't go any further. You may get a phone call from someone on Wednesday next week, and I'll give you a reference number, and we'll talk about." We're sort of setting the scene of the sympathetic approach. (Tony, Corporate Ombudsman, expert)

These quotes are examples of how IWRs suggest to whistleblowers that they will be safe because they can remain anonymous; the IWR will care for them by ensuring this. Concerning line managers as trustors, signaling benevolence seemed difficult:

> How it [suggesting to managers that people feel unable to raise a concern in their team] is framed and how it is acted on and how difficult that is for those middle managers and often senior manager to be told negative information [by the IWR] and then not feel that it reflects on their own self-concept. (James, Regulator, expert)

Often, IWRs had difficulty in approaching managers with information about potential malpractice under their supervision without them feeling attacked or betrayed. In this sense, IWRs struggled to be regarded as 'of service' to line managers.

There were also instances where IWRs explained how they signal integrity to whistleblowers and line managers. Towards whistleblowers, IWRs emphasized communication:

> The first reply [to potential whistleblowers] is that we take this and every matter seriously and we will look into it, and we will give a feedback. (Mohammed, General Counsel, engineering)

To managers it was by emphasizing the value of the process:

> If I look into the cases that arise in the organization, whenever I have a case and it looks a little bit like corruption, the HR colleagues do not like it if I give them to the compliance organization. [...] I can say, "If we don't give it to them, and the case escalates, then we are part of the problem. Please let's be part of the solution and not part of the problem." And this is what the colleagues always understand. (Hannah, HR Lead for Speak-up, engineering)

The IWR explains here that managers sometimes need to be encouraged to keep their hands off a report and let others—the compliance team—handle it, in line with the proper process and principles. The message is that following the process is 'the solution'.

At times, interviewees mentioned barriers to signaling trustworthiness that related to time, more precisely the passing of time:

> We have been trying to become-- to build a culture which is much more adult-to-adult than the patriarchal culture that used to exist in this sector. (Dave, Investigator, bank)
>
> In the beginning we were mostly considered as police. More and more they see you as a trusted advisor, because of frequent interactions. (Jose, Compliance Latin America, engineering)
>
> We have a plan, but it needs time [to implement it]. It is because [we want to] change employees' mind-set from fearful to brave. [We want to] change employees' mind-set that the [whistleblowing system] is useful for the organization as well as for them personally. (Jasmine, Secretary, government)

These examples illustrate how IWRs use the various dimensions of trustworthiness in trying to convince internal stakeholders that the channels they operate are trustworthy. This often boils down to conveying themselves as trustworthy operators and function holders of the whistleblowing channels and systems. The IWRs seem to be signaling trustworthiness emphasizing different attributions depending on the perceived needs of the respective trustor (whistleblower, line manager, top management). The implication is that IWRs often find themselves in situations where they are sending out inconsistent and sometimes even contradictory trustworthiness signals. I refer these as synchronic tensions when this concerns different stakeholders simultaneously, or diachronic tensions when the same stakeholder across time is concerned. Although the four organizations studied were different (in terms of their management structures as well as the longevity of speaking up arrangements in place), we found that challenges and possibilities for IWRs to signal trustworthiness attributes relate more to the whistleblowing process itself than to the structure of the organization in which they might occur. Let's look at these in a bit more detail.

3.2.2 Synchronic Tensions

Signaling a particular trustworthiness attribute to one stakeholder can contradict the signaling of the same or another trustworthiness attribute to another stakeholder. The implication of such synchronous tensions is that the challenges IWRs face to be perceived as trustworthy organizational actors stem partially from the different stakeholder expectations they need to cater for simultaneously.

One example is the tension of signaling different abilities to whistleblowers and to top management. An ombudsperson noted that, as a whistleblowing recipient, their trustworthiness depended on their ability to listen to both employees and to top management but that this listening ability involved tension.

> The ombudsman should be open to anything, really. Anything that the whistleblower thinks is best positioned in this line of communication for example because it didn't fit anywhere else. (Tony, corporate ombudsman, expert)

> [An organization] would not want to pay an ombudsman to listen to [employee concerns] forever, so to speak, literally. And then carry all that stuff back inside. (Tony, corporate ombudsman, expert)

In the ombudsman's words, for a whistleblower a competent IWR means being able to make management listen. For top management however, a competent IWR is someone who filters out concerns about issues that top management might not consider important enough.

Another example relates to the ability of an IWR to derive various statistics from the database of whistleblowing concerns—proof that they were listening 'endlessly'—was a key aspect of signaling to top management an ability to control internal whistleblowing activity.

> So people can't say they didn't know how to raise an issue with management [...] It's dead easy, dead straightforward, no excuses, please, please get that to me. (Mike, HR Director, hospital)

For this IWR, high numbers of whistleblowing concerns meant that the would-be whistleblowers took the internal channels seriously. However, it does not tell as much if the recipients of the information can listen to employees' concerns. While it was clear for the IWRs that top managers consider numbers important, IWRs themselves had doubts about what the numbers were actually telling.

> Is more or less [whistleblower reports] a good sign or a bad sign? If there was none [no whistleblower had used the channel], I'd be really worried. If there was nobody writing to the CEO, I would be really worried. I don't want us to get to the extreme - one of the models we looked at where every single thing that an employee could ever possibly raise is counted in their whistleblowing. And it's not the culture I'm trying to encourage. (Nataliya, operational lead for speak-up, bank)

Internal whistleblowing systems are typically founded on a promise of no retaliation against a whistleblower. In the following quote, the IWR refers to text in whistleblowing policy that the organization will not tolerate retaliation against an employee who reports through the whistleblowing channel. This is part of a range of commitments IWRs make and signal.

> There are commitments in the fact that if there's substance it will be investigated. That confidentiality would be maintained. The individual who raises the issue will receive some communication to let them know - the outcome. Whether actions been taken or not been taken etcetera. (Nataliya, operational lead for speak-up, bank)

We can see here that objectivity ('it will be investigated'), protection ('confidentiality'), and follow-up ('feedback') are core principles of how the organization will interact with the whistleblower. However, further in the interview the IWR suggests that this signaling of integrity to whistleblowers immediately impedes the signaling of benevolence to line managers:

> [...] it's still challenging in terms of how do you say to a manager, "Have you heard about the wrongdoings that are happening in your department?" Because it's just such a loaded question. (Nataliya, operational lead for speak-up, bank)

These quotes illustrate the difficulty of being an impartial IWR. A vital function of the IWR is to neutralize an employee's potential lack of trust in line managers to maintain the employee's trust in the organization, i.e., if you cannot trust your line manager you can still trust the whistleblowing channel. However, the way in which the IWR commits the handling of the reports is felt—by the same IWR—as making them less trustworthy to other stakeholders, such as the line managers in whose departments alleged wrongdoing occurs.

3.2.3 Diachronic Tensions

The contradictory signaling of trustworthiness attributes does not only occur when the IWR feels compelled to cater to different stakeholder expectations simultaneously. There are also tensions and contradictions in signaling trustworthiness to the same trustor at different stages in the whistleblowing process. Hence, besides synchronic tensions, there are also tensions across time or diachronic tensions. This was most visible in relation to the confidentiality of a whistleblower's identity.

The promise that the whistleblower's identity will be kept confidential is made as a signal of trustworthiness in training (attribution of integrity) and, at the initial stage of the whistleblowing process, to obtain sufficient information from the employee about the alleged wrongdoing (reassurance as attribution of benevolence). One of the IWRs we interviewed even met the whistleblower in secrecy outside the office.

However, once a concern gets to the investigation stage, keeping the whistleblower's identity confidential becomes problematic:

> I don't think it can be as anonymous as you'd like to think. It would definitely not be talked about openly, but - you know the thing about "I told everyone to keep it a secret." So, there'll be whatever would be involved. Which you'd always have, if you involved the committee, and the investigation team, compliance or whoever, the HR team. At least 15 people. (Beatrice, policy lead for speak-up, bank)

Whistleblowing scholars and policy experts also note the difficulty in maintaining confidentiality in disclosure processes required for adjudication and corrective action. Some of our interviewees tried to pre-empt this tension during the initial contact with the whistleblower.

> We had to write the individual to say, "Look, for us to progress this it will involve us passing it over to the work force performance team. Therefore, they will know your name and whatever else [...]." (Esther, HR manager, bank)

While having initially signaled trustworthiness by promising confidentiality, this promise was moderated when an employee actually raised a concern with the IWR, who explained to the employee that others might guess who the whistleblower was.

The IWR would also, after informing the whistleblower of the risk of being identified, ask the whistleblower for advice on how best to investigate the claim to minimize the risk of identification.

3.2.4 Think About How You Signal Trustworthiness

The point I am trying to make by showing you these quotes and my analysis using the ABI-model, is to encourage thinking carefully about how to signal the trustworthiness of internal whistleblowing channels and of those who operate them. Using the different dimensions of trustworthiness allowed me to understand and explain why IWRs can feel impelled to signal trustworthiness to different internal stakeholders in contradicting and self-undermining ways.

The synchronic tensions I provide some illustrations of, mainly stem from different expectations stakeholders have, related to their specific position and roles within the organization. As such, I do not believe it is ever possible to fully resolve these synchronic tensions. Important is to be aware this is going on rather than panic about it. Nevertheless, these tensions might be lessened if it is possible to invite different stakeholders to some perspective taking, i.e., imagining what the expectations of the other stakeholders are towards internal whistleblowing channels. Stakeholder positions come with stakeholder interests, but it is useful and helpful if there is some appreciation of the interests that other stakeholder positions entail.

The diachronic tensions I pointed at tend to stem from a mistake IWRs often make with regard to the time frame that matters here. It seems that often IWRs see no other option than to over-signal at the beginning. They tend to promise too much in order to get someone to use the channel. These promises cannot be kept, and this further undermines the work of making the whistleblowing system trustworthy. Whilst many IWRs I speak to seem to understand very well that this is a problem, very few have had the courage to take the long term view in building trustworthiness. What they do is signal the principles of the handling process, commit to them, but also inform potential whistleblowers of the limitations in confidentiality and protection that they can offer. In the end, these IWRs and the systems they operate, come out as more trustworthy because they do not have to scale back their earlier promises and signaling.

References

Cabana, G. C., & Kaptein, M. (2021). Team ethical cultures within an organization: A differentiation perspective on their existence and relevance. *Journal of Business Ethics, 170*, 761–780.

Edmondson, A. (1999). Psychological safety and learning behavior in work teams. *Administrative Science Quarterly, 44*(2), 350–383.

Hardin, R. (2002). *Trust and trustworthiness*. Russel Sage Foundation.

Kannan-Narasimhan, R., & Lawrence, B. S. (2012). Behavioral integrity: How leader referents and trust matter to workplace outcomes. *Journal of Business Ethics, 111*, 165–178.
Kaptein, M. (2008). Developing and testing a measure for the ethical culture of organizations: The corporate ethical virtues model. *Journal of Organizational Behavior, 29*(7), 923–947.
Kenny, K., Vandekerckhove, W., & Fotaki, M. (2019). *The whistleblowing guide: Speak-up arrangements, challenges and best practices*. Wiley.
Mayer, R. C., Davis, J. H., & Schoorman, F. D. (1995). An integrative model of organizational trust. *Academy of Management Review, 20*(3), 709–734.
McEvily, B., Perrone, V., & Zaheer, A. (2003). Trust as an organizing principle. *Organization Science, 14*(1), 1–106.
Möllering, G. (2006). *Trust: Reason, routine, reflexivity*. Elsevier.
Pirson, M., & Malhotra, D. (2011). Foundations of organizational trust: What matters to different stakeholders? *Organization Science, 22*(4), 1087–1104.
Rothschild, J., & Miethe, T. D. (1999). Whistle-blower disclosures and management retaliation: The battle to control information about organization corruption. *Work and Occupations, 26*(1), 107–128.
Rousseau, D. M., Sitkin, S. B., Burt, R. S., & Camerer, C. (1998). Not so different after all: A cross-discipline view of trust. *Academy of Management Review, 23*(3), 393–405.
Vandekerckhove, W., & Phillips, A. (2019). Whistleblowing as a protracted process: A study of UK whistleblower journeys. *Journal of Business Ethics, 159*(1), 201–219.
Vandekerckhove, W., Fotaki, M., Kenny, K., & Özdemir Kaya, D. D. (2025). Signalling trustworthiness of internal whistleblowing channels in organizations: Temporality matters! *Organization Studies*. https://doi.org/10.1177/01708406251317262

Wim Vandekerckhove is (Full) Professor of Business Ethics at EDHEC Business School in France. He holds a PhD from Ghent University. Before joining EDHEC, he has held academic affiliations to Ghent University (Belgium), the University of Oslo (Norway), Griffith University (Australia), the International Anti-Corruption Academy (Austria), and the University of Greenwich (UK). Wim has been Editor-in-Chief for *Philosophy of Management*, and is currently Consulting Editor for the *Journal of Business Ethics*. Wim has provided expertise to various organizations, including Council of Europe, United Nations Office on Drugs and Crime (UNODC), the International Olympic Committee (IOC), Transparency International, the UK Department of Health, the UK Financial Conduct Authority. He is a committee member of the British Standards Institute (BSI) on governance. He led the development of ISO37002:2021, the international standard for Whistleblowing Management Systems, and participated in developing BS25700 Organizational Responses to Modern Slavery.

Chapter 4
Listening Cultures

Abstract This chapter presents research into the cognitive barriers for speak-up cultures. I analyze how integrity professionals make sense of the whistleblowing channels and of whistleblowers to identify two sets of epistemological and axiological assumptions, one of listeners and another set of those who disperse others' speak-up. I use interview data with those who oversee internal whistleblowing channels in English hospitals. I provide corroboration for my sets of assumptions from NHS staff survey data.

4.1 From Speak-Up to Listen-Up

In October 2022, the House of Commons in the UK published the Kirkup Review (Kirkup, 2022). Following concerns about the quality and outcomes of maternity care at East Kent University Hospital Trust, Dr Kirkup was asked to lead an independent investigation into a suspiciously high mortality rate of new-borns in two hospitals of the East Kent Trust. His report from that investigation—the Kirkup Review—found that with a different management culture at the hospitals, 45 babies would have lived (70% of the suspicious deaths). One of the key culture-problems at the hospitals, according to the report, was the failure throughout the hospital to pick up signals, a failure to listen. For example, Kirkup writes that midwifes 'described ineffective communication and discussions [in which] decisions come from the top, rather than because staff communicate well and listen to each other' (p. 77), and that 'midwifes were not listened to and were not taken seriously when concerns were raised' (p. 79).

Kirkup also notes that what the investigation found in East Kent was not a 'one-off, isolated failure, a freak event that "will never happen again"' (p. v). Rather, since 2015, he had seen an increase in policy initiatives directed at maternity services, yet, since then there had also been major service failures. For Kirkup there was a clear pattern. It was in 2015 that Sir Robert Francis published the Freedom to Speak Up Review (Francis, 2015), also an independent investigation into whistleblower detriment in the National Health Service (NHS) in England. Toward the end of 2014, I had been commissioned by the Department of Health to carry out research that was

W. Vandekerckhove, *Whistleblowing Management Systems and Speak-Up Cultures*, SpringerBriefs in Business, https://doi.org/10.1007/978-3-032-14204-7_4

used for the Francis report (or the F2SU as it is often called). Reading the Kirkup Review at the end of 2022, and noting the devastating consequences of the lack of listen-culture, I revisited my data from 2014. This chapter presents my further analysis of that data. The F2SU had led to a new role within the NHS. Each NHS Trust had a F2SU-guardian (mostly a part-time role or just on top of other duties) and these were networked and supported through a National F2SU Guardian Office. The Kirkup Review was the ultimate confirmation of previous critiques on that F2SU structure. It wasn't working.

As part of that research, I had analyzed the quality of whistleblowing policies of NHS Trusts, but had not found a correlation with staff survey responses. I had also interviewed whistleblowers and recipients of whistleblowing in the NHS (HR managers, medical directors, and case handlers). The report from that commissioned research distinguished two groups of recipients: on the one hand recipients who actively engaged with staff when they 'spoke up' or raised concerns, and on the other hand recipients who had no trust in whistleblowing because they saw so many problems with whistleblowers. I decided to revisit the recipient interview data and approach it from a specific theoretical lens, in order to gain more insight into what the epistemology of listening is in the context of 'picking up the signals' about malpractice in an organization. If it is not the organizational policy and not the organization role or structure, then might it be someone's assumptions about knowing, warning, and responding that makes a listen-culture?

The theoretical lens I used to re-analyze the interview data is that of 'negative capabilities'. French (2001) and Simpson et al. (2002) introduced this to organization studies as an aspect of leadership crucial in the context of change management. The concept denotes a specific listening epistemology. Having explored instances of negative capabilities in an M&A project, Simpson and French (2006) call for research that explores implications and gives detailed descriptions of negative capability in other specific fields of application. This chapter does that for internal whistleblowing. More precisely, this chapter develops a structure for sets of assumptions that distinguish a listener from a non-listener. Through my analysis, I suggest that these sets consist of two epistemological assumptions (method for knowledge, and sources of knowledge) and two axiological assumptions (control of other, and control of self) that enables people to 'read the signals', or not.

I'm grateful to Nataliya Rumyantseva, with whom I conducted the initial research. We were colleagues at the time, at the University of Greenwich. Our original report is in the UK Government Web Archive (Vandekerckhove & Rumyantseva, 2015). After we published it, we spent hours discussing how we might theorize further as to how a listening culture differed from a non-listeners culture. It was Nataliya who brought my attention to the notion of 'negative capability'. By then however, each of us were on different projects and both of us eventually left Greenwich. I provided her with a draft of what later became this chapter—any mistakes remain mine of course. The chapter is structured as follows. I first discuss 'negative capabilities' as a theoretical lens for the analysis. Then follows a short methods section. This is followed by a section in which I present and discuss the findings of the analysis. The chapter concludes with a short summary.

4.2 Negative Capability Versus Dispersion

French (2001) used the concept 'negative capability' to denote an aspect of leadership, which he deemed crucial in the context of change management. Cornish (2011) elaborates on the components of 'negative capabilities' being 'open mindedness, attentiveness to diversity and the suspension of the ego' (p. 135). Change inevitably arouses emotions, regardless of the scale of change or whether change is deliberate or unexpected. This, French argues, is because situations of change are ambiguous, i.e., they involve risk-taking and working without full knowledge. Negative capability 'indicates the capacity to live with and to tolerate ambiguity and paradox' (French, 2001: 482). It denotes a non-defensive way to engage with change; not merely reacting but rather adapting, shifting, and adjusting as necessary 'to allow one's mind to be changed by others' (ibid).

Etymologically, 'capacity' is derived from the Latin *capax*, meaning 'able to hold much'. Since empty space is able to hold much, 'negative' denotes emptiness, or not full. Part of what leaders need to be able to do is 'containment', 'taking in' the emotions 'evoked by a situation' (French, 2001: 484). French picked up the notion of 'negative capability' from psychoanalysts Bion and Eisold, who in turn lent it from the poet Keats. For Eisold (2000, p.65) it is 'precisely the ability to tolerate anxiety and fear, to stay in the place of uncertainty in order to allow for the emergence of new thoughts or perceptions'. Simpson et al. (2002) use this notion to analyze leadership in the context of a merger between North-American, Russian, and Chinese companies. They describe how the American manager involved in the yearlong negotiations developed the 'capacity to hear the meaning that are often obscured as much as revealed by words, and then to convey them to others' (Simpson et al., 2002: 1217).

It is possible to use this description also for the situation whistleblowing recipients find themselves in. Whistleblowing is 'the disclosure by organization members [...] of illegal, immoral or illegitimate practices under the control of their employers, to persons or organizations that may be able to effect action' (Near & Miceli, 1985, p.4). The act of whistleblowing is a call for change. Yet, perhaps more so than the standard definition suggests, it is often unsettling and induces uncertainty. Communication from whistleblowers is often confused (De Graaf, 2019). Is a vexatious tone an indication of frustration from earlier attempts to reason directly with one's line manager, or of malice? Is an exaggerated implication of a minor omission on someone's part a sign of an aggrieved worker or of expertise? If the whistleblower says the alleged wrongdoing has been going on for months, then why is the concern raised only now? If it reads like someone venting, is it just that or is the whistleblower communicating the broader team dynamic that may be toxic? Research in Australia and New Zealand (Brown et al., 2019) suggests that not all reports can be neatly categorized as reports of clear integrity breaches (28%) or clear personal grievances (30%). The biggest group (42%) were reports that included various elements.

Simpson et al. (2002) make reference to Stein's (1994) deep listening skills of the organizational consultant, who listens for the hidden story to emerge. It is in this way that the leader becomes an instrument for organizational inquiry and learning.

In the context of the arising 'unknown', which inevitably emerges when an act of whistleblowing is performed, the managers' reliance on routine professional knowledge and expertise alone (which Cornish calls positive capabilities) may be less relevant than the ability to handle uncertainty and engage with reality 'in its full and diverse concreteness' (Cornish, 2011). The qualities that are helpful here include 'receptive expectation' toward the source of ambivalence (e.g., whistleblowers) and high levels of self-awareness that facilitates not only maintaining one's focus but also consistently noticing where one's focus lies and how (and if) it changes. Another helpful concept I borrow from Cornish is 'user-centered approach' or in the context of the current chapter, the whistleblower centered approach. Where one's focus must primarily lie when confronted with a whistleblower concern, is with the person's speaking and the concern they are raising, not with the whistleblower's suspected motivations or possible detrimental consequences to the organization. By focusing primarily on the nature of the concern and how, in the NHS context, it relates to patient care, 'underpinned by empathy and creativity' (Cornish, 2011) a recipient of a concern would be promoting the culture of openness and receptivity advocated for by both the Francis (2015) report as well as the Kirkup Review (Kirkup, 2022).

As Cornish discusses this in relation to social workers, it is not simply knowing what to look for but knowing how to look, 'this includes seeing the particular details which no generic toolkit, however comprehensive, can include, and being open to framing what is seen in far greater complexity than a checklist can incorporate' (p. 140). Hence negative capabilities cannot be fully codified in organizational policies or training manuals. They have to be embodied and enacted every single time a manager is confronted by a whistleblowing event. Clearly, such careful, empathetic, and attentive responses need to be supported by the wider organizational culture.

Forgas and George (2001) argue that situations of high complexity, ambiguity, and uncertainty require substantive processing, and it is in these situations that emotions are most likely to impact our cognition. For this reason, leadership scholars have turned to emotional intelligence in order to understand and moderate these effects (e.g., Ashkanasy & Ashton-James, 2005). Research suggests that emotional competencies (Salovey & Mayer, 1990) relate to self-control, which is crucial for developing empathy and listening skills. This form of self-control, i.e., stopping one's instant reactions and generating time is akin to what Fisher and Ury (1981) called the 'step back, go to the balcony' strategy in negations. Being able to do this helps in not reacting defensively but rather act toward an affirmative solution.

Simpson and French (2006) however suggest the notion of 'negative capability' entails a broader view of working with emotion than what we can find in the literature on emotional intelligence in a leadership context. That stream appears to be preoccupied with repairing negative emotions or functional uses of emotions (George & Zhou, 2002). More precisely, what is not emphasized enough in the emotional intelligence literature is the importance of 'just being there' and 'just listening' (Simpson and French, 2002), what Cornish calls 'heightened receptivity to reality in its full and diverse concreteness' (p. 141).

Part of negative capabilities is 'holding back from a premature understanding and interpretation of what we experience, which necessitates the suspension of the active intellect which seeks to categorize and therefore limit what it finds' (Cornish, 2011, p. 143). At the same time, it would be wrong to suggest that the literature on negative capability prescribes inaction. On the contrary, it acknowledges that 'immediate work needs to be done' (Simpson & French, 2006), i.e., actions and interventions stemming from positive capability, by which French (2001), Simpson et al. (2002), and Simpson and French (2006) understand the skills and competencies in applying learned frameworks of analysis and making decisions. Negative and positive capabilities are complimentary, not opposites. While positive capabilities are exercised as usual, negative capabilities 'provide the space within which lack of clarity and understanding can be tolerated and lead to there being space for new insights rather than precipitate action' (Cornish, 2011, p. 144). Negative capabilities are a precursor to informed action, not an alternative to it. Leaders need to intend, expect, and plan (positive capability) but also see or hear when one can no longer rely on what one knows or on relationships one believed to have developed (Simpson et al., 2002). One then needs to be 'available for thoughts that are present in the emotional matrix of organizational experience' (Simpson & French, 2006, p. 246), and be able 'to find thought that are available but as yet do not have a thinker' (ibid). Cornish associates negative capabilities with the negation of the ego, whereas the opposite of negative capabilities is acting out of ego. 'Central here is the practitioner's readiness to demonstrate humility, identifying with others where they are, rather than imposing their own ego and default ways of working' (p. 144). This approach to management goes against the mainstream managerialist expectations for managers to act promptly and decisively. Clearly drawing on negative capabilities by managers in the NHS context requires wider organizational support, training, and encouragement.

Lacking negative capability, not being able to do the containment work, a finer analysis of emergent realities and acting out of ego can results in pre-mature actions which in the context of high ambivalence can quickly turn into patterns of avoidance and defenses against the unknown (the whistleblower). These are precisely the kinds of responses that are often experienced by whistleblowers (Rotschild & Miethe, 1999; Kenny, 2019). In other words, the lack of negative capabilities in whistleblowing recipients can turn out to be a costly oversight for the organization. French (2001) applies the term 'dispersal' to further explain how managers act when confronted with ambivalence and uncertainty but lack negative capabilities to handle it constructively. Namely they give examples of forms of dispersal found in the context of change management. These are: (1) emotional dispersal (e.g., tears of anger, frustration, fear) that although vents the emotions does not lead to constructive outcomes or resolution of the problem and may generate additional problems, (2) explanations (e.g., telling and retelling the organizational history to explain current arrangements and problems) without achieving constructive changes, and (3) activity (e.g., every doubt was met by a new project, a new demand, a new initiative) which appears useful but does not lead to substantive improvement of outcomes.

Simpson et al. (2002) and Simpson and French (2006) call for research that explores implications and gives detailed descriptions of negative capability in specific fields of application. This chapter develops a description of epistemic and axiological assumptions of negative capability in the context of internal whistleblowing.

4.3 A Listening Epistemology and Axiology

This chapter uses interview data from a broader project on speak-up arrangements in NHS Trusts in England. For that broader project semi-structured interviews were conducted in September and October 2014 with 37 people (14 whistleblowers, 15 managers, and Directors, 8 respondents with a specific expertise external to the Trusts).

The interviews were audio-recorded and transcribed verbatim. Transcripts were sent to interviewees for review and amendment. Individuals and organizations were anonymized at the point of transcription. Interviewees and corresponding Trusts were given a numeric code. All identifying information was destroyed upon completion of the project at the end of 2015.

For this chapter, only the transcripts from the interviews with the 15 managers and Directors were used. These were HR managers, HR Directors or Medical Directors who had an oversight or operational role in the organization's speak-up channels and process.

From the thematic analysis of the interviews with recipients, two sets of assumptions emerged, with which the recipients narrated how they responded to people who raise a concern. These are presented in Tables 4.1 and 4.2. Some theory driven codes were used, which allowed me to cast one set as 'negative capability' (Table 4.1) and the other as 'dispersion' (Table 4.2).

Table 4.1 Epistemology and axiology of negative capability (theory driven codes with *)

	2nd order themes	1st order themes	Codes
Negative capability	Knowledge	Method	Listening
			Conversation
			Open to broader view
			Postpone judgement*
			Non-verbal
		Locus	Thought without a thinker*
			Emerging knowledge
			Emerging decision
			Beyond policies
			Not using external knowledge
			Not using external categories
	Control	Other	Accepting other's phrasing*
			Open to be influenced by others
		Self	Limited control
			Limited own knowledge

Table 4.2 Epistemology and axiology of dispersion (theory driven codes with *)

	2nd order themes	1st order themes	Codes
Dispersion	Knowledge	Method	Explanation
			Robust monitoring
		Source	Superior knowledge
			We are clear
			Reliance on external definition
			Reliance on external categorization
	Control	Other	Profiling of other
			Denial of other's phrasing*
			Order never fails
			No noise allowed
		Self	Superior leader
			Own ability
			Denial of failure
			Speed
			Action before communication

First and second order themes reveal a similar structure and indicate that negative capability consists of both epistemic as well as axiological assumptions. The epistemic assumptions relate to how a recipient comes to know something (method) and where that knowledge emanates from (locus/source). Axiological assumptions relate to notions of control over others and over self. In this section I follow that structure to present and discuss the findings.

Epistemic assumptions

In talking about how they responded to staff who raised a concern, recipients mentioned epistemic notions. These were assumptions of how they come to know something about the concern (method) or about the person raising it, as well as the location of that knowledge (locus/source).

With regard to method, some recipients were explaining how the concerns weren't really concerns but merely a side-effect of an organizational feature. They were explaining it away. They saw an underlying reason for the concerns, which those who raised the concern did not see. One recipient also insisted knowing about all concerns raised because they had such robust 'live time' monitoring of staff concerns. These method-codes were categorized as dispersion.

The codes allocated to the negative capability set revealed a different method to knowledge about staff concerns. Recipients mentioned that it was important not to rush to judgement and instead postpone judgement so that one can take appropriate decisions. Often the concern that was raised would be just one of a number of issues or concerns the person had. Hence, one had to be open to that broader view from which a person was raising their concern. Recipients acknowledged that someone might feel that they've responded to a concern but that actually they failed to hear what the person was saying and thus the person does not feel listened to. Hence, recipients acknowledged that listening was not straightforward and unproblematic, but rather requires having conversations and attending to non-verbal communication, such as body language.

With regard to the locus or source of knowledge, the codes grouped under the dispersion theme denote instances where recipients saw themselves as the source of knowledge about the dynamics of raising a concern. This included recipients who were convinced of their superior knowledge to identify and categorize concerns easily. They also had a definition at hand of what a whistleblower was. It also included recipients who repeatedly said how clear they actually were in their response to those who raise a concern, or how clear the organization's policy was. Often in those instances, recipients would also mention fixed categorizations established external to interactions with staff or the hospital. These external determinations were always cast as hierarchical (e.g., NHS or the law) and it was the recipient who held the expertise, acting as the medium of knowledge for the organization.

The codes for locus of knowledge in the negative capability set are quite different. To start with, some recipients avoided using externally established categories or definitions. In their experience these external instruments are blunt and do not fit with what they felt was needed. There were instances where recipients said they had made a conscious decision to depart from those external instruments and work beyond the policy (note: NHS hospitals are obliged to have a whistleblowing policy with a mandatory minimum content). For them, the policy wasn't where the real work was in getting to hear people's concerns. Rather, what needs to happen emerges from the conversation with the person who raises the concern. Knowledge that can be acted upon does not rest within a policy, a speaker, or a recipient but instead emerges from an interaction that is actively sought, through conversation and through triangulation of different inputs. Some recipients described their role as a mediator, or a translator of what the person raising a concern could not articulate. The literature mentions negative capability as the ability to grasp a thought that does not have a thinker yet, and there were instances in the data that illustrated this really well. This is not the same as explaining away someone's concern. Rather, in grasping a 'thought without a thinker' one does acknowledge the concern someone raises but is able to see the whole iceberg of which the raised concern was merely the tip.

Axiological assumptions

The thematic analysis also revealed two juxtaposing axiological assumptions, which allow to characterize notions of control of others and self as pertaining to either negative capability or dispersion.

With regard to self-control, instances that pertain to a negative capability position include recipients indicating they did not know—sometimes explicitly—and having only limited control of a situation, in the sense that one might plan to get concerns raised in a certain way or through a specific channel, but you need to take into account that it won't happen that way. Instances in the data that were coded as such were from recipients who indicated being comfortable with such a lack of control.

Codes relating to self-control that were more characteristic of dispersion were used for instances in the data where recipients bestowed themselves with superior leadership or as a role model, and held a firm belief in their own ability to have full control over a situation. On the rare occasion that handling a report or responding to a concern goes wrong, recipients would sometimes deny the failure was on their part. Instead, they would emphasize the speed at which they were able to respond and react when a concern was raised. Their quick resolving of issues entailed taking action first and then communicating with the person who had raised the concern. This is a stark contrast to instances of negative capability, in which recipients actively seek to start or prolong the conversation before making decisions.

With regard to control of others, the codes grouped under the negative capability heading denote instances where recipients indicated that their approach was whistleblower centered, meaning that they were accepting the person's phrasing of a concern. It indicates that these recipients were trying to understand how someone had experienced a situation that led them to raise a concern. Resonating with that were instances in which recipients indicated to be allow those who raise a concern to influence the decisions and actions in response to the concern. This included seeing different viewpoints as beneficial, but also bringing the person who had raised to concern to the table in designing the organizational response, i.e., making the whistleblower part of the team that resolves the problem.

The dispersion codes for control of others denote a quite different axiological position. Often, when narrating how they respond to concerns that are raised, recipients were profiling those who had raised a concern, as troublemakers, as frustrated employees, or as people who try to game a system. There were also instances where recipients would invalidate how someone had phrased their concern, and simply assert that the person had actually meant something totally different. What also suggested a control of others was recipients' insistence on order. They were convinced their response system worked really well. Even when there were frictions, these would not endanger the smooth running of that neatly ordered system. In that sense, order never failed. Instances where it would fail are merely noise and thus, irrelevant to how the response system was arranged and operationalized.

Robust sets of assumptions

The grouping of the codes under first and second order themes, as well as attributing to the resulting sets of assumptions the headings 'negative capabilities' and 'dispersion' worked well conceptually. But would it work to characterize someone as a listener or a non-listener, based on their narrative of how they respond to staff concerns? Figure 4.1 shows a mapping of how interviews were coded to the first order themes. On the left-hand side is the set of epistemic and axiological assumptions of the negative capability set, with the first order themes (method, locus, control over others, self-control). On the right-hand side is the set of dispersion assumptions, which has the same structure of epistemic and axiological first order themes. In the middle is the list of interviews (#1-#15), and for each interview lines are drawn indicating to which set of first order themes the codes in the interview data were grouped.

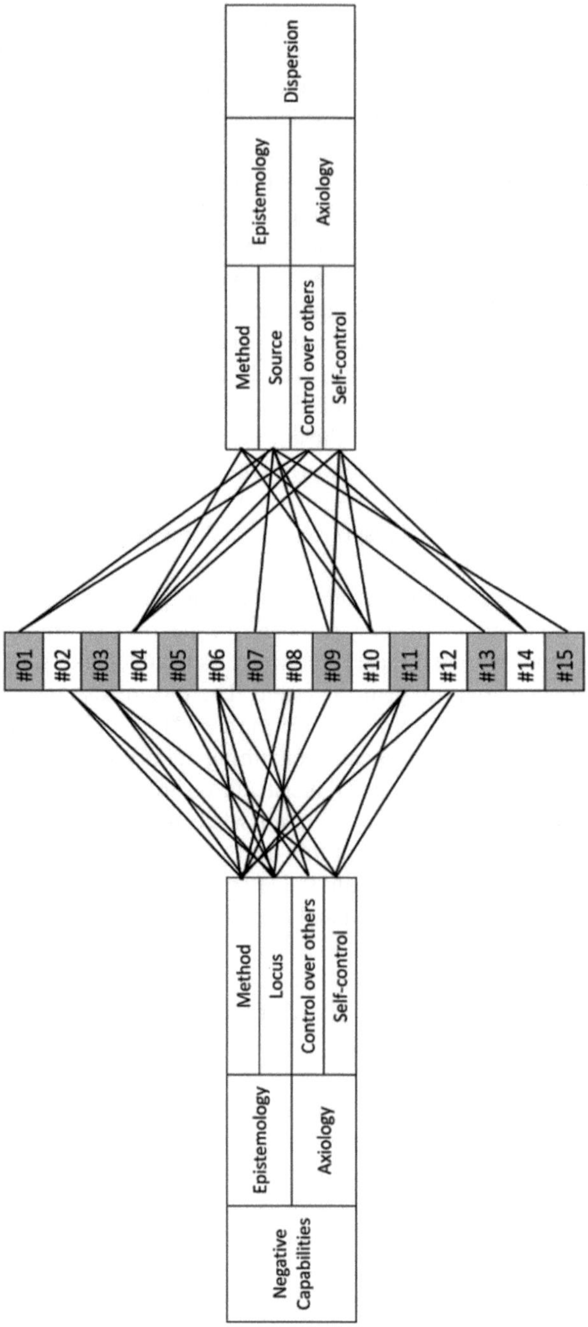

Fig. 4.1 Interview coding alignment

We can make two observations about Fig. 4.1. The first is that each first order theme included coding from at least two different interviews. Hence, themes are recurrent across different people. The second observation is that interviews tend to be easily characterizable as either espousing negative capabilities or dispersion. Of the 15 interviewees, 7 had coding that was exhaustively grouped in the negative capability set, and 6 had coding that was exhaustively grouped in the dispersion set. Only two of the interviewees had coding that went both into the negative capability as well as the dispersion set. This suggests that the constructs of negative capability and dispersion as sets of epistemic and axiological assumptions are not only conceptually sound but also empirically robust.

To get a further indication of the robustness of our juxtaposition of 'negative capability' and 'dispersion' attitudes in managers, we used data from the NHS Staff Survey 2015. The idea was to see whether differences we see in those who are supposed to listen (cf. our interview data from managers) are corroborated by how those who are supposed to be speakers experience the organizational culture (cf. NHS Staff Survey results). Figure 4.2 shows plots of how the 10 Trusts score across the five retained items from the NHS Staff Survey. These items were: '8b) Communication between senior management and staff is effective', '8c) Senior managers here try to involve staff in important decisions', '8d) Senior managers act on staff feedback', '12c) When errors, near misses or incidents are reported, my organization takes action to ensure that they do not happen again', '12d) We are given feedback about changes made in response to reported errors, near misses and incidents'. These are indeed aspects of management culture for which one would expect our distinctions between 'negative capability' and 'dispersion' to make a difference for staff experience. For NHS Trusts of which we had characterized an interviewee NHS manager as 'negative capability', the staff survey shows a higher score than for NHS Trusts where our manager characterization was 'dispersion'. There is one exception. One of the dots on the '1' column is consistently lower than the others in that column, and across the five diagrams shows a pattern similar to that of the dots in the '2' column. This represents an NHS Trust from which we interviewed three managers, of which one was characterized as 'negative capability' and two as 'dispersion'. This might suggest that it is not enough for just one manager or director to have 'negative capability' but it needs to be characteristic for the tone at the top.

We see that the distinction between the two sets of assumptions derived from our qualitative analysis of interview data with managers and directors, is corroborated by independently gathered staff survey data. We believe this corroboration between our manager data (interviews) and staff data (relevant staff survey items) is a further indication of the robustness of the sets of epistemic and axiological assumptions emerging from our analysis.

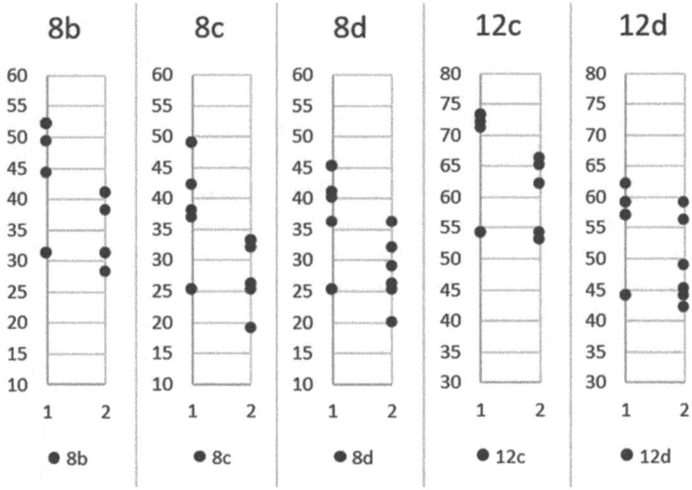

Fig. 4.2 Corroboration of interview based grouping with NHS Staff Survey items. *Note*: On the *X*-axis, '1' denotes negative capability and '2' denotes dispersion. The *Y*-axis are percentages of NHS Trust staff that responded 'Agree' or 'Strongly agree' to the 2015 NHS Staff Survey items indicated at the top of each diagram. The items are: 8b) Communication between senior management and staff is effective, 8c) Senior managers here try to involve staff in important decisions, 8d) Senior managers act on staff feedback, 12c) When errors, near misses or incidents are reported, my organization takes action to ensure that they do not happen again, 12d) We are given feedback about changes made in response to reported errors, near misses and incidents

4.4 Listening Culture Is Not a Self-Administered Scale

I believe our findings presented in the previous section are important, both in terms of theoretical contribution as well as practical implication. French (2001) introduces the concept of negative capability to management scholarship and offers anecdotal illustrations of both negative capability as well as dispersal. Simpson et al. (2002) offer illustrations from a single case (international negotiations); Simpson and French (2006) provide a mainly conceptual and philosophical discussion of negative capability. Hence, the research presented in this chapter contributes to the management scholarship on negative capability by developing negative capability and dispersion as constructs of opposing epistemic and axiological assumptions. This development is done inductively across different interviewees from a similar setting, i.e., recipients of staff concerns in hospitals in England.

The findings further suggest that the two sets of assumptions are robust across different people. Only two of our 15 interviewees showed indications of both negative capability as well as dispersion assumptions. The other 13 were consistently coded as either negative capability or dispersion. This suggests that the constructs developed in this research might be used for developing better listeners and hence ethical management. We have at our disposal at the moment two well developed and validated constructs that can be used as a proxy for speak-up/listen-up cultures—the organizational cultures where for Kirkup the signal would be read—namely psychological safety (Edmondson, 1999) and discussability (Kaptein, 2008).

Psychological safety is the extent to which people believe others will not reject them for saying what they think and that others are interested in people as people, which leads people to voice their concerns and seek feedback. It is based on Edmondson's (1999) approach to organizational learning which held that learning does not depend on specific structures or actions from the top but rather requires an 'ongoing process of reflection and action, characterized by asking questions, seeking feedback, experimenting, reflecting on results, and discussing errors or unexpected outcomes of actions' (p. 353). Kaptein (2008) defines discussability as 'the opportunity employees have to raise and discuss ethical issues' (p. 926). This construct is further operationalized as the perceived scope employees have to 'exchange, analyze, and discuss their experiences' (p. 927), so that they can 'learn from others' (near) mistakes, transgressions, and dilemmas' (p. 927).

While the research presented in this chapter has led us to suggest a construct of negative capability, we do not, like Edmondson (1999) and Kaptein (2008) validate a scale to quantitatively measure it. Our research nevertheless makes an important contribution. Both psychological safety as well as discussability measure a situation from the perspective of speakers. The contribution the research presented in this chapter makes is that negative capability and dispersion can be seen as constructs for evaluating a situation from the perspective of the listener. More precisely, we suggest that the set of epistemic and axiological assumptions of negative capability characterizes the attitude managers need to take as listeners if they want psychological safety or discussability to be the outcome.

We also need to discuss our construct of negative capability vis-à-vis an extant construct that does approach openness to other views from a listener's point of view. Davis (1980) developed 'perspective taking' as a validated scale in an attempt to develop constructs that allow to measure the multidimensional nature of empathy. The perspective taking scale provides for a measure of the cognitive dimension of empathy, through seven items that 'assess spontaneous attempts to adopt the perspectives of other people and see things from their point of view' (Davis, 1980: 2). We believe that conceptually there is a substantial overlap between Davis' perspective taking scale and the development of a negative capability construct, which our research contributes to. There remain important differences, however. First, the perspective taking scale items use wording to denote a general cognitive tendency, while our work on negative capability shows what such a general tendency might look like for a specific context, i.e., attitudes of listening to whistleblowers. Davis' scale items use wording that seems more appropriate for a private rather than a professional context, e.g., item 3: 'I sometimes try to understand my friends better by imagining how things look from their perspective', or item 7: 'When I'm upset at someone, I usually try to "put myself in his shoes" for a while' (David, 1980: 7, our emphasis).

Second, the perspective taking scale is a self-scoring instrument, whereas what I develop in this chapter on negative capability is a model that can be used by researchers and consultants to assess managers' cognitive tendencies for listening by analyzing their narrative accounts of how they work. As a self-scoring instrument, the perspective taking scale assumes a respondent is self-aware about their (lack of) perspective taking, for example in item 5 of Davis' scale: 'I sometimes find it difficult to see things from "the other guy's" point of view' (reverse scored). Such an assumption is not necessary when using the epistemology and axiology we identified in our research for negative capability and dispersion, because these can be used to analyze someone else's account of their experiences with handling whistleblower reports. For example, most of the managers we characterized as 'dispersion' would have been convinced they knew precisely what the other's point of view was, and even believed they knew it better than those others (e.g., our codes 'profiling other', 'explanation', 'denial of other's phrasing').

Third, pending further research, we believe it plausible to assert that acting with negative capability requires a high level of perspective taking, hence negative capability is a broader concept. Extant research corroborates so, but at the same time offers good reasons to explore this further in future research. Rupp et al. (2008) conducted a field study among bank tellers and found that a low level of perspective taking correlates with perceiving customer injustice, i.e., believing that customers behave unfairly toward oneself. This is similar to what we thematized as dispersion's axiological assumption by managers that the whistleblower is either incapable or abusing the procedure, rather than something being wrong with the procedure itself. The latter would be an axiological assumption of managers acting with negative capability.

However, extant research also corroborates our suggestion that our emerging negative capability construct is broader than that of perspective taking. Cojuharenco and Sguera (2015) examined the role of perspective taking on how acceptable individuals find it to lie in order to protect their company, and whether that effect interacted with time pressure, measured as 'perceived hurriedness'. They find that when individuals feel less pressed for time, perspective taking inhibits the acceptability of lying but that is not so when individuals feel more in a hurry. In the context of handling a whistleblower report, time pressure may be important. In that sense, it is interesting to note that not experiencing time constraints as pressure, or as hurriedness, is a key aspect of negative capability. Eisold (2000) described it as 'to stay in the place of uncertainty', and French (2001) wrote that negative capability indicates the 'capacity to live with and to tolerate ambiguity'. Thus, acting with negative capability implies one does not jump to conclusions and does not act out of sense of pressure. This also emerged from our data. One of our respondents spoke of the speed at which they went through the process, including making decisions and taking action before communicating with the whistleblower. We assigned this coding as part of the dispersion attitude. The findings of Cojuharenco and Sguera (2015) support our code assignment, as well as our suggestion that negative capability might be more encompassing than perspective taking. Ability to resist pressure when a situation requires speedy decisions forms an aspect of negative capability but not of perspective taking.

Further corroboration can be found in Grant et al. (2017) who studied effects of leadership coaching in an Australian healthcare context. The study used perspective taking as a dependent variable, showing an increase in perspective taking as one of the positive outcomes of leadership coaching. Interestingly, ambiguity tolerance also increased and was assessed separately from perspective taking. Ambiguity tolerance is a key aspect of negative capability (French, 2001) and the fact that Grant et al. (2017) does not assume it included in the perspective taking construct, corroborates our suggestion that negative capability is broader than perspective taking.

4.5 Researching Listening Attitudes

A recurrent theme in whistleblower stories is that managers just wouldn't listen. This chapter uses interview data to provide insights into what characterizes a listener attitude. The interviewees had an oversight or operational role in the speak-up channels and processes in their organization. The theoretical lens of 'negative capability' was used to identify sets of epistemic and axiological assumptions that correspond with respectively listener and non-listener attitudes. Findings suggest both sets have a similar structure. Epistemic assumptions include how a recipient comes to know something (method) and where that knowledge emanates from (locus/source). Axiological assumptions include notions of control over others and over self.

While further research is needed, the characterization of listener and non-listener attitudes developed in this chapter might be used in conjunction with concepts of psychological safety and discussability. These latter constructs approach speak-up/listen-up cultures from the point of view of speakers. The negative capability construct developed in this chapter—although still at a preliminary level—approaches such cultures from the point of view of the listener.

Further research is also needed to explore the conceptual overlap between negative capability and perspective taking. Both allow the research of listening attitudes from a listener's point of view. The work presented in this chapter on negative capability opens new possible research designs and as a construct negative capability might encompass more aspects than perspective taking.

References

Ashkanasy, N. M., & Ashton-James, C. E. (2005). Emotion in organizations: A neglected topic in I/O psychology, but with a bright future. *International Review of Industrial and Organizational Psychology, 20*, 221–265.

Brown, A. J., Lawrence, S., Olsen, J., Rosemann, L., Hall, K., Tsahuridu, E., Wheeler, C., Macaulay, M., Smith, R., & Brough, P. (2019). *Clean as a whistle. A five step guide to better whistleblowing policy and practice in business and government*. Retrieved January 31, 2023, from https://www.whistlingwhiletheywork.edu.au/

Cojuharenco, I., & Sguera, F. (2015). When empathic concern and perspective taking matter for ethical judgment: The role of time hurriedness. *Journal of Business Ethics, 130*(3), 717–725.

Cornish, S. (2011). Negative capability and social work: Insights from Keats, Bion and business. *Journal of Social Work Practice, 25*(2), 135–148.
Davis, M. H. (1980). A multidimensional approach to individual differences in empathy. *JSAS Catalog of Selected Documents in Psychology, 10*, 85.
De Graaf, G. (2019). What works: The role of confidential integrity advisors and effective whistleblowing. *International Public Management Journal, 22*(2), 213–231.
Edmondson, A. C. (1999). Psychological safety and learning behavior in work teams. *Administrative Science Quarterly, 44*, 350–383.
Eisold, K. (2000). The rediscovery of the unknown: An inquiry into psychoanalytic praxis. *Contemporary Psychoanalysis, 36*(1), 57–75.
Fisher, R., & Ury, W. (1981). *Getting to yes: How to negotiate without giving in*. Arrow.
Forgas, J. P., & George, J. M. (2001). Affective influences on judgments and behaviour in organizations: An information processing perspective. *Organisational Behavior and Human Decision Processes, 86*(1), 3–34.
Francis, R. (2015). *Freedom to speak up review*. Department of Health. Retrieved 7 February, 2023, from http://freedomtospeakup.org.uk/the-report/
French, R. (2001). Negative capability": Managing the confusing uncertainties of change. *Journal of Organizational Change Management, 14*(5), 480–492.
George, J. M., & Zhou, J. (2002). Understanding when bad moods foster creativity and good ones don't: The role of context and clarity of feelings. *Journal of Applied Psychology, 87*(4), 687–697.
Grant, A. M., Studholme, I., Verma, R., Kirkwood, L., Paton, B., & O'Connor, S. (2017). The impact of leadership coaching in an Australian healthcare setting. *Journal of Health Organization and Management, 31*(2), 237–252.
Kaptein, M. (2008). Developing and testing a measure for the ethical culture of organizations: The Corporate ethical virtues model. *Journal of Organizational Behavior, 29*(7), 923–947.
Kenny, K. (2019). *Whistleblowing: Toward a new theory*. Harvard University Press.
Kirkup, B. (2022). *Reading the signals. Maternity and neonatal services in East Kent – the report oft he independent investigation*. Department of Health and Social Care. Retrieved 7 February, 2023, from https://www.gov.uk/government/publications/maternity-and-neonatal-services-in-east-kent-reading-the-signals-report
Near, J. P., & Miceli, M. P. (1985). Organizational dissidence: The case of whistle-blowing. *Journal of Business Ethics, 4*(1), 1–16.
Rothschild, J., & Miethe, T. D. (1999). Whistle-blower disclosures and management retaliation: The battle to control information about organization corruption. *Work and Occupations, 26*(1), 107–128.
Rupp, D. E., McCance, A. S., Spencer, S., & Sonntag, K. (2008). Customer (in)justice and emotional labor: The role of perspective taking, anger, and emotional regulation. *Journal of Management, 34*(5), 903–924.
Salovey, P., & Mayer, J. D. (1990). Emotional intelligence. *Imagination, Cognition and Personality, 9*(3), 185–211.
Simpson, P., & French, R. (2006). Negative capability and the capacity to think in the present moment: Some implications for leadership practice. *Leadership, 2*(2), 245–255.
Simpson, P., French, R., & Harvey, C. (2002). Leadership and negative capability. *Human Relations, 55*(10), 1209–1226.
Stein, H. (1994). *The dream of culture*. Psyche Press.
Vandekerckhove, W., & Rumyantseva, N. (2015). *Freedom to speak up—Qualitative research report*. Retrieved September 25, 2025, from https://webarchive.nationalarchives.gov.uk/ukgwa/20150218150343/https://freedomtospeakup.org.uk/wp-content/uploads/2014/07/Freedom_to_Speak_Up_-_Qualitative_Research_Report.pdf

Wim Vandekerckhove is (Full) Professor of Business Ethics at EDHEC Business School in France. He holds a PhD from Ghent University. Before joining EDHEC, he has held academic affiliations to Ghent University (Belgium), the University of Oslo (Norway), Griffith University (Australia), the International Anti-Corruption Academy (Austria), and the University of Greenwich (UK). Wim has been Editor-in-Chief for *Philosophy of Management*, and is currently Consulting Editor for the *Journal of Business Ethics*. Wim has provided expertise to various organizations, including Council of Europe, United Nations Office on Drugs and Crime (UNODC), the International Olympic Committee (IOC), Transparency International, the UK Department of Health, the UK Financial Conduct Authority. He is a committee member of the British Standards Institute (BSI) on governance. He led the development of ISO37002:2021, the international standard for Whistleblowing Management Systems, and participated in developing BS25700 Organizational Responses to Modern Slavery.

Chapter 5
Conclusion

Abstract This chapter concludes this book on internal whistleblowing systems and speak-up cultures. It summarizes the key points made throughout the chapters, pivoting from operating formal channels for people to speak up to subconscious biases toward those who speak up. Ultimately, the quest is for an ability to listen.

This book started with guidance for operating effective whistleblowing channels in organizations, derived from three normative benchmarks: the ISO37002:2021 standard for whistleblowing management systems, the 2022 ICC Guidelines on whistleblowing, and the requirements of the EU Whistleblowing Directive (2019/1937) for organizational whistleblowing channels. The guidance is intended for integrity professionals, which is anyone who is tasked with designing, implementing, operating, or overseeing whistleblowing channels in organizations. That chapter also explained how SUSA works, the free online and anonymous tool I developed for integrity professionals to self-assess how an organizational whistleblowing channel aligns with those three normative benchmarks.

Although SUSA is not designed as a research tool, we can do some research based on data from the SUSA tool. I presented some findings from an analysis that uses a SUSA sample from the first year SUSA was operational. These findings suggest organizations have the channels in place but remain poor at giving feedback to those who report wrongdoing through those channels. The findings on data privacy aspects in handling processes were also worrisome. A further disconnect appears to exist between having a mandated function for supporting and protecting the whistleblower on the one hand, and a credible organizational capacity for providing adequate protection and remedy on the other hand.

The SUSA findings on governance indicators showed coherence between the strength of the whistleblowing officer mandate. This will be no surprise for integrity professionals or scholars. These indicators also showed to be associated with attention to diversity and inclusion, an area that not only remains under-researched, but that also remains surprisingly sensitive with integrity professionals.

In chapter three, the book pointed at further gaps and disconnects between a formal box-tick and an engagement to make a whistleblowing system responsive. It

W. Vandekerckhove, *Whistleblowing Management Systems and Speak-Up Cultures*, SpringerBriefs in Business, https://doi.org/10.1007/978-3-032-14204-7_5

was my starting point to discuss the possible but not so evident relationship between organizational whistleblowing channels and organizational speak-up cultures. The use of whistleblowing channels can indicate a lack of psychological safety within teams, or loss of trust in a direct manager. Whistleblowing channels require trust at the organizational level. They can help to build trust at the team level only if whistleblowing channels are managed as a system, which means in a PDCA cycle of continuous improvement.

The SUSA data suggests this is not happening in most organizations. It indicates poor management when whistleblowing channels are operated without having a documented process for evaluating the channels, and without relying on indicators to monitor the whistleblowing system's performance. These findings led me to suggest that whistleblowing officers are often lonely in the sense that all responsibility for operating the channels, handling reports and being responsive to those who raise a concern, falls on them. That is not how speak-up cultures are built.

In chapter three I also discussed research on how integrity professionals attempt to signal the trustworthiness of the organizational whistleblowing system. Internal stakeholders—workers, middle managers, and top management—have very different expectations, and many integrity professionals struggle to accommodate these.

In chapter four I used the notion of 'negative capability' to distinguish listeners from non-listeners. I revisited data collected on an earlier project with integrity professionals in hospitals. The notion 'negative capability' refers to the ability to tolerate uncertainty and allow the emergence of new thoughts and perceptions. It is the leadership skill of not jumping to conclusions, and is a necessary requirement for deep listening.

I used that notion to identify a listening epistemology and axiology. That concludes the travel in this book. Starting from formal aspects of whistleblowing channels, the book pivoted a systems approach for continuous improvement as the way to start building speak-up cultures and organizational capacity for trustworthiness. Ultimately however, a speak-up culture depends on the ability to listen. This book is not about the whistleblowers, not about those who speak. Rather, the book is about our repeated failures to listen to them. It was written in the hope we might get better at listening.

Wim Vandekerckhove is (Full) Professor of Business Ethics at EDHEC Business School in France. He holds a PhD from Ghent University. Before joining EDHEC, he has held academic affiliations to Ghent University (Belgium), the University of Oslo (Norway), Griffith University (Australia), the International Anti-Corruption Academy (Austria), and the University of Greenwich (UK). Wim has been Editor-in-Chief for *Philosophy of Management*, and is currently Consulting Editor for the *Journal of Business Ethics*. Wim has provided expertise to various organizations, including Council of Europe, United Nations Office on Drugs and Crime (UNODC), the International Olympic Committee (IOC), Transparency International, the UK Department of Health, the UK Financial Conduct Authority. He is a committee member of the British Standards Institute (BSI) on governance. He led the development of ISO37002:2021, the international standard for Whistleblowing Management Systems, and participated in developing BS25700 Organizational Responses to Modern Slavery.

MIX
Papier aus verantwortungsvollen Quellen
Paper from responsible sources
FSC® C105338

If you have any concerns about our products,
you can contact us on
ProductSafety@springernature.com

In case Publisher is established outside the EU,
the EU authorized representative is:
Springer Nature Customer Service Center GmbH
Europaplatz 3, 69115 Heidelberg, Germany

Printed by Libri Plureos GmbH
in Hamburg, Germany